HORRIBLE Canadian HISTORIES

CLAIRE MACKAY
First Folks
and
Vile Voyageurs

Illustrated by
BILL DICKSON

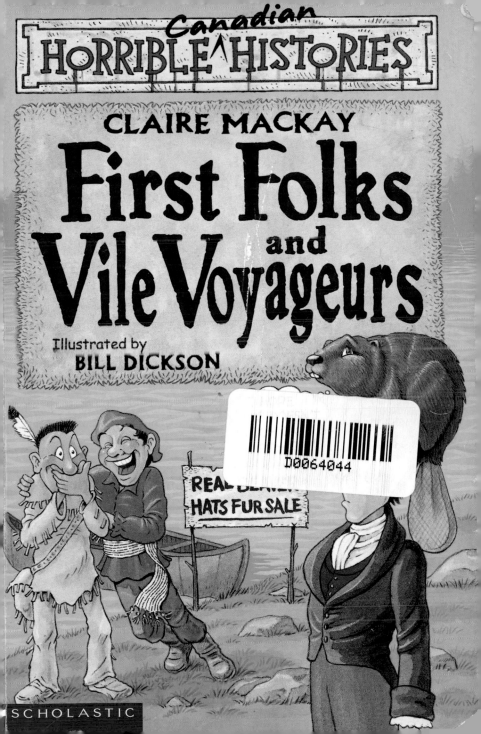

READ ~~BEAVER~~ HATS FUR SALE

D0064044

SCHOLASTIC

First Folks
and
Vile Voyageurs

Claire Mackay

Illustrations by
Bill Dickson

Scholastic Canada Ltd.
New York Toronto London Auckland Sydney
Mexico City New Delhi Hong Kong

Scholastic Canada Ltd.
175 Hillmount Road, Markham, Ontario L6C 1Z7, Canada

Scholastic Inc.
555 Broadway, New York, NY 10012, USA

Scholastic Australia Pty Limited
PO Box 579, Gosford, NSW 2250, Australia

Scholastic New Zealand Limited
Private Bag 94407, Greenmount, Auckland, New Zealand

Scholastic Publications Ltd.
Villiers House, Clarendon Avenue, Leamington Spa,
Warwickshire CV32 5PR, UK

Illustration page 158 based on illustration from *The 26 Letters*, by Oscar Ogg

National Library of Canada Cataloguing in Publication Data

Mackay, Claire, 1930–
First folks and vile voyageurs

(Horrible Canadian histories)
ISBN 0-439-98857-8

1. Canada — History — Juvenile humour. I. Dickson, Bill. II. Title.
III. Series: Mackay, Claire, 1930– . Horrible Canadian histories.

FC173.M32 2001   j971'.002'07   C2001-930274-6
F1026.4.M32 2001

5 4 3 2 1   Printed in Canada   01 02 03 04 05

*To Pat Hancock, for friendship,
for commiseration,
and for most of the sources used
in this book*

I owe thanks to many, including Janet Lunn for clearing the underbrush; Joan Clark for some glittering chips off the Rock; Gilles Plante for being rude to me in French; Hank Hancock for going the extra fathom;
Virginia Euwer Wolff for a delicious and unforgettable phrase;
Laura Peetoom for searching out errors with the devoted scrupulosity of a tickbird on a hippo; Kahente Horn-Miller for a fast and fascinating intro to Mohawk; and Sandy Bogart Johnston and Diane Kerner for taking a chance on an aging writer.

Scholastic gratefully acknowledges the original inspiration of Terry Deary's hugely hilarious *Horrible Histories* series published by Scholastic Publications Ltd, London, UK.

TABLE OF CONTENTS

WARNING!

If send-ups get you down, stop right now and read no further. We've poked fun at *everyone* in this book. Nobody who is *anybody* in Canadian history has been spared.

The Opening Bit

History can be horrible. Horribly boring. Especially Canadian history. Some people think Canadian history is more boring than watching water freeze. Some people think Canadian history *is* watching water freeze. Other people think there isn't any Canadian history. When they hear the words "Canadian history" they fall over laughing, the way they do when they hear "airline food" or "painless dentistry" or "military intelligence" — or "tasty

broccoli." (Such expressions are oxymorons. If you don't know that word go look it up in that big book over there. It's called a dictionary. It has lots of words in it.) Others say that Canadians are too polite to have any history. These people seem to think history is how many creatures you murder and how many trees you chop down. When you read this book you'll find out that Canadians can murder creatures and chop down trees perfectly well, thank you very much. It's just that they usually apologize first, eh?

So read on.

Sorry about that.

CRABBY CHRONOLOGY I

The dates below are just good guesses, give or take a century or two. Or maybe three. As far as we know, nobody wrote stuff down — or we haven't dug up their Daytimers yet.

80,000 B.C. Last Ice Age starts. Sea level drops 120 metres (about the height of a 30-storey building). Land bridge from Asia to Alaska pops up. Herds of mastodons, woolly mammoths, musk oxen and double-humped camels amble across, along with hordes of giant sloths, bison, horses and shortfaced bears (whatever they might be). The critters turn themselves into a supermarket. And seriously huge beavers show up, too, as big as a Volkswagen, with an overbite you wouldn't believe. They turn themselves into a national symbol.

20,000 B.C. (maybe way earlier; maybe way later) People come the same route, take a look at the ice and head south. First known sighting of snowbirds.

13,000 B.C. Niagara Falls starts to fall.

10,000 B.C. Ice heads north. So do people. They spread all over the place.

8000 B.C. It gets warmer. More folks arrive to hunt mastodon and mammoth in the prairies and Arctic. Just before the land bridge vanishes underwater, the last batch of people cross over from Siberia. They are hotshot makers of stone tools.

7000 B.C. A good mammoth gets hard to find. Folks switch to caribou, follow herds on the Arctic mainland. **Back east** in Labrador and on the Atlantic coast, the ancestors of the Beothuk, Mi'kmaq and Maliseet arrive from the south.

4000 B.C. People start making neat stuff out of copper, especially around Lake Superior. A bustling continental commerce — the first North American free trade? — flourishes. Knives, dart heads, awls, chisels, fish hooks, needles and ornaments change hands a lot.

2000 B.C. Folks from Alaska move into the High and Eastern Arctic to hunt whales, seals and caribou. They make skin-covered boats (*umiaks*), harpoons, and bows and arrows. Clever bunch. Another group, living in the Hudson Bay area, in Labrador and in the northern forests, devises kayaks, whale-oil lamps and igloos. Clever bunch. They also have tame dogs. Which are pretty clever, too.

JUST ONCE, YOU COULD STAY HOME AND HELP YOUR MOTHER MAKE THE DISHES BEFORE YOU GO OFF HUNTING WITH THE BOYS!

1000 B.C. People start making neat stuff out of clay,

especially in southern Ontario and New Brunswick. Pots, pans, bowls and cups — made by women because they do all the cooking, of course — are everyday items.

500 B.C. Some tribes of First Folks grow and use tobacco, mostly for trade and ritual purposes.

0 Nothing happens. (Besides, nobody has thought of zero yet: "the number that, when added to another number, equals the second number." Way cool.)

A.D. 125 Early Woodland tribes begin to bury dead relatives — after a few days this is usually a good idea — on a bluff above a lake near Peterborough.

A.D. 300 They finish burying relatives. (No, not the same ones!) By now the bodies are piled up in a snake-shaped mound, 60 metres long and nearly 2 metres high. Big mucky-mucks — chiefs and shamans and elders — are tucked neatly around the base, rabble scattered through the rubble. No surprise there. White guys dug it up a while ago (white guys do this a lot) and named it Serpent Mound. No surprise there.

A.D. 500 The natives in southern Ontario settle down and start to grow stuff. Soon corn is as high as an elephant's eye.
Chinese monk Hoel Shin writes a book about visiting "Fusant," a country that sounds like British Columbia.

A.D. 560 Irish monk Brendan (later Saint Brendan) the Navigator conducts Mass on top of a whale in the middle of the Atlantic, finds an island full of birds that speak Latin, and discovers Newfoundland. Or so the story goes.

A.D. 900 Folks calling themselves *Inuit* ("the people") spread eastward from Alaska, into all regions of the Arctic, Baffin Island and Labrador, pushing out an ancient tribe they named *Tunit* ("the people earlier than us"), a.k.a. Dorsets. During the next 200 years the Tunit dwindle to zip, leaving behind beautiful miniatures of bears, seals, shaman wands and dead relatives.

A.D. 985 Eric the Red hunkers down in Greenland. Bjarni Herjolfsson accidentally sees North America.

A.D. 1000 Leif Ericsson and friends land on North America.

FIRST FOLKS

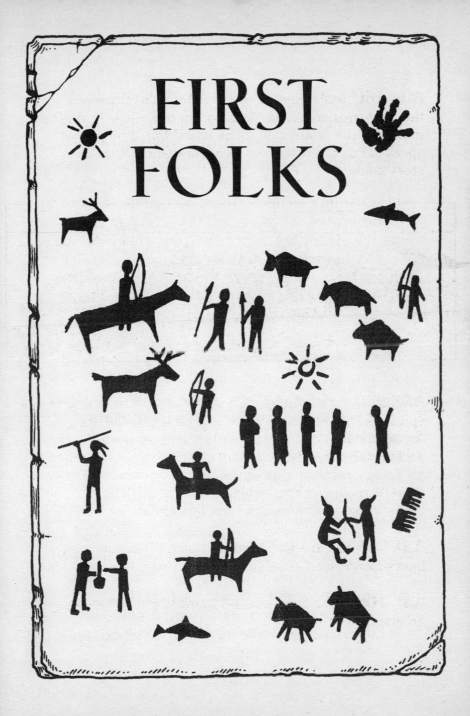

A thousand years ago, close to half a million people lived in Canada, from sea to shining sea to shining sea. Dozens of tribes and tribelets spoke dozens of different languages and dialects. The west coast types didn't understand the east coast types. (They still don't.) The northerners couldn't talk to the southerners. What's more, they thought the southerners were a bunch of wusses. (They still do.) Were a Mohawk to talk to a Mi'kmaq, or a Chinook to a Chipewyan, or a Blackfoot to a Beothuk — or vice versa — none of them would talk back. But all had things in common:

1. They lived off whatever their little piece of the planet provided, whether animal, vegetable or mineral.

2. They believed in one or more supernatural beings.

3. They told stories.

4. They made art and music.

5. They loved games, gambling and children, not necessarily in that order.

For example: Let's suppose you live way up north in the Arctic Barrens. It's winter, several hundred years ago. The weather outside is frightful. You need some shelter. You look around. Unlike the three little pigs, you have no straw, no wood, no

bricks. What do you have? Snow. In fact, more snow
than you really need. So okay, you build a house out
of snow. And there you are, sitting around in a box
of frozen water. Which, when you think about it, is
pretty amazing. You call it an *iglu*, which to you
means "dwelling."

It's dark inside, though, and still a bit chilly.
So you go outside and find a chunk of stone. It
happens to be soapstone, the softest stone in the
entire stone family. Lucky you. You make a little
pan-like thing out of it, and throw in a hunk of fat
from the seal you caught last week. Now you need
a wick. Dead easy. A flock of Canada geese, clever
creatures, just took off for the south. They left you
a present — a couple of hundred kilograms of dung.
In fact, more dung than you really need. But perfect
for wicks. You get out your fire-drill kit — a sharp
stick or bone, a piece of driftwood with a hole in it,

a hunk of dry moss — and rub the stick back and forth between your hands on the driftwood, fast, until the moss starts to burn. Light the goose dung and — *SHA-ZAM!* You can see right across the room, and you're warm as toast — even if you have no idea what toast is. You take off your parka (made out of the seal you captured last year), and your mukluks (made out of the seal you captured last month — in fact, *mukluk* means "seal"), and you ask, "What's for supper?" Your family looks at you as if you have blubber for brains, and says, "Pizza!" (Just kidding — the answer is: The seal you captured yesterday. Ask a sealy question, get a sealy answer.)

After supper it's quality time. Your uncle tells a story of the sea-goddess Sedna, She-Who-Must-Be-Obeyed, who has power over the weather and the seal supply, and who knows when you are bad or good. Or perhaps a tale of the Great White Bear, whose spirit must be soothed by gifts, especially after you kill him. Your grandmother is up on the sleeping platform, making a flat drum from a whale's stomach. Meanwhile, you carve away at a soapstone walrus, or maybe a seal, and your two little cousins — naked as peeled apples, even though they don't know what an apple is — play a game called Guess How Many Stones Are in the Hand Behind My Back, and if You Don't Guess It Right You Get a Little Whack. (It's longer in Inuktitut.)

And so, for each tribe throughout the vast country, life depended on the bounty of earth and water around them.

South of the Inuit, in the Subarctic, the Dene relied on the caribou for food, clothing, tools and shelter. Ditto for the Cree around Hudson Bay, with the odd moose for variety. (And there are few things odder than a moose.) On the west coast, the daily

special for the Tlingit, Haida and Kwakiutl was salmon. On the prairies, where roamed the Blackfoot (Siksika), Assiniboine and Sioux, the staple of life was the buffalo. (This buffalo wasn't really a buffalo, it was a bison. Real buffaloes live in Africa and Asia.) Around the Great Lakes, the Iroquois and Huron grew maize (Indian corn), beans and squash, and hunted deer, rabbit and wild fowl. In the east the Mi'kmaq, Maliseet and Beothuk lived on fish, moose and the odd oyster. (And there are few things odder than an oyster. One of them is a moose.)

Dependent as they were on all of nature, it's no surprise that the First Folks had an enormous reverence for it. They believed that everything — sun, moon, tree, rock, porcupine, duck, catfish — had a spirit and deserved respect. (Even the mosquito, which is really pushing the envelope.) Nature also deserved offerings, and sometimes sacrifice. And they had a whole gang of gods and godlets, as fascinating, as powerful, and as mean and tricky as those of the ancient Greeks.

For instance: Top god for many Algonquin tribes was *Gitchi Manitou*, Great Spirit or Great Mystery or Master of Life (*manitou* means "soul" or "essence," which exists in all things). He was a good guy. The bad guy was *Matchi Manitou*, and if he got you . . .

bummer, man! You'd end up "under the earth in
a wretched dungeon swarming with serpents [to]
endure every degree of misery." Tricksters like *Napi*
and Coyote lied, stole and played tricks on the
Blackfoot, but they also showed the people how
to behave. Raven did the same to the Pacific coast
tribes and Inuit, but he also gave them light, the fire
drill and women. Uh-huh. There were giants, too.
Nanabozho of the northern forests got mad one
day and shook his blanket, whereupon a hundred
islands appeared. *Glooscap*, warrior-magician of the
Mi'kmaq and Maliseet, had a pillow that turned into

Prince Edward Island. Then there was the terrifying *Wendigo*, a nightmarish creature who lurked in the woods hungering for human flesh.

Another thing the native tribes had in common — like people anywhere — was fighting. Out west the seagoing Haida raided villages up and down the coast. The Tlingit made slaves of the Salish, who often went to war with the Blackfoot. Down east the Mi'kmaq fought with the Montagnais and Inuit north of the St. Lawrence River, with the Iroquois to the west and with the Algonquin to the south. Then they helped the French and English (*Mi'kmaq* means "allies") wipe out the poor Beothuk, who didn't fight with anybody except a couple of Vikings. The Tunit were probably killed off by the Inuit, who were in turn often raided by the Cree. The Cree fought with the Blackfoot, who fought with the Assiniboine, who fought with the Sioux, who fought with the Ojibwa, who fought with the Iroquois, who fought with everybody in sight.

Any questions? If so, keep them to yourself.

WHY DO WE SAY IT?

bury the hatchet: to make peace, call a truce, end a quarrel. When native tribes wished to put an end to fighting, a hatchet was buried deep in the ground, with great ceremony.

First Names

The First Folks named many of Canada's animals. Good thing, too, or we'd be saying, "Look! There's a big/small/medium-sized brown/black/striped critter!" instead of "Look! There's a . . . ":

caribou, from Mi'kmaq *halibu*, pawer, scratcher; literally, snow shoveller

chipmunk, from Ojibwa *atchitamon*, head first — how a chipmunk or a squirrel goes down a tree. (The first all-Canadian airplane was called a Chipmunk, too — which is pretty scary.)

moose, from Cree *moosoa*, browser, stripper (of leaves! Stop that giggling!)

raccoon, from Algonquian *ara'kunem*, he scratches with his hands

skunk, from Abenaki *seganku*, skunk; but earlier from Algonquian *sekakwu*, where *sek-* means urinate and *kwu* means fox. (You're giggling again!)

FASHIONS FROM THE FIRST FOLKS

Some of the items we wear come from the First Folks:

mackinaw: a coat or shirt of heavy cloth, for outdoor wear, from Mackinaw, Michigan, an early trading post and fort attacked by British troops in the War of 1812. They ran out of overcoats, so got some cloth from the fort and made jackets. "Mackinaw" is one spelling of the Algonquian word *mackinac*, turtle. The land nearby is shaped like the shell of a turtle.

parka: from Aleutian *purka*, skin, outer coat; originally from the Samoyed (native people of Siberia) word meaning hide or pelt. A thigh-length hooded coat used by Russian fur traders in Alaska.

mukluk: from Yupik (western Inuit) *maklak*, bearded seal; traditional winter boot of sealskin

or caribou, now also made by white guys in the south. (Note: do not confuse with *muktuk*, from Inuit *maktak*, the outer skin of the whale, a favourite delicacy of the northern people. You eat it raw and it tastes like hazelnuts.)

moccasin: from Algonquian *makasin*, also Mi'kmaq *m'cusun*, a flat-soled shoe or boot of soft leather.

tuxedo: This is complicated, so pay attention. Please. Back in 1886, in a trendy resort town north of Manhattan, it was time for the rich people to hold the big fall dance. Pierre Lorillard, the richest of the rich, wanted to wear something a little different. His tailor designed a black jacket without tails, but Pierre chickened out the night of the dance. His son wore it instead — launching a multimillion-dollar industry. Soon the jacket was called a tuxedo, taking its name from the town (and country club) where it was first worn, Tuxedo Park. So what? you say. Well, a couple of centuries earlier, a wandering tribelet of the St. Lawrence Algonquin lived there, whose chief was called *P'tuksit*, meaning wolf — literally, "he has a round foot." (The *p* is silent, by the way, as in *p*terodactyl. Or swimming.) To honour him, the tribe gave their camp the same name. After the white guys swiped the land, around 1765, they marked it on the map as Tucksito. Tuxedo — get it? White guys spell with forked tongue.

17

THE LEGEND
OF DEKANAHWIDĖH

There came a time (maybe in the fifteenth century, but nobody really knows) when the Iroquois stopped fighting, at least for a while. Here's the story:

1. A young Huron woman living near the Bay of Quinte gets a message, in a dream, from the Creator. (Does this sound familiar?)

2. She is told she will be the virgin mother of a great hero. (This too?)

3. She has a son and names him Dekanahwideh, the Heavenly Messenger (even though his name means either "two rivers come together" or "double row of teeth." Maybe both.)

4. When he grows up, he tells his mother he's on a mission — to bring "the good news of peace and power" to the world. (She doesn't call 911.)

5. He takes his mother to a tree on a hill near Lake Ontario and tells her to come there each year and hit the tree with a hatchet. If blood flows, it means he failed; if sap, he succeeded.

6. He crosses the lake in a stone canoe, which is the First Miracle, and decides to test his power. He goes to the cabin of a killer/cannibal, where he climbs up on the roof and looks down the smoke hole so his reflection shows in the pot of water on the fire.

7. The killer comes home ready for some tasty boiled human, looks in the pot and sees the strong, noble, kind, etc., face of Dekanahwideh. Well! He is alone, he thinks, so the face must be his own. He is stricken with shame at the contrast between what he *should* be — strong, noble, kind, etc. — and what he *is* — a nasty merciless cannibal.

8. Dekanahwideh walks in and makes his sales pitch (peace and power). Killer/cannibal is converted on the spot, says, "Right on! I'm your man!" and becomes the first disciple. (Second Miracle.)

9. They start spreading the word to bring nations together so "the land shall be beautiful, the river shall have no more waves, one may go everywhere without fear." But . . .

10. Big problem is the seriously ugly and wicked Onondaga super-chief Atotarho, whose body is twisted seven different ways and who has live snakes in his hair. (Every day's a bad hair day.)

11. Dekanahwideh gives a new name to ex-cannibal/disciple, Hiawatha, meaning "He Who Combs," and says that one day Hiawatha will comb snakes out of Atotarho's hair, and peace will reign.

12. They carry the message to the Mohawk, the Oneida, the Cayuga, the Seneca. Dekanahwideh pulls off a couple of miracles to convince the scoffers. He climbs a tall tree, commands it to be chopped down, and falls to certain death in the deep river below, only to be found on the riverbank the next morning cooking his breakfast. Then he orders the sun to go out. It does. (Lucky for him there was an eclipse in 1451.) Warriors from all four tribes follow him into the land of the Onondaga and the evil Atotarho. Atotarho takes one look at the multitude, does a complete one-eighty and joins up, whereupon Hiawatha combs the snakes out of his hair. Atotarho's still ugly, though.

13. Dekanahwideh plants "the Tree of Peace, a great white pine with white roots" which reach north, south, east and west over all the earth, to guide people in the ways of peace. An eagle flies above the tree, watching for any danger. Below the tree, Dekanahwideh fashions a cave in which are buried forever all the weapons of war.

14. Dekanahwideh puts antlers on the heads of fifty men, appointing them chiefs. He tells them that if a Wind (war) should come, and the Tree of Peace is uprooted, they are to seek a great swamp elm. Beneath it they will find shelter. Then he bids them farewell and disappears into history.

The five-nation alliance lives on, becoming six when the Tuscarora ("hemp gatherers") — those few who survive a dreadful massacre by white colonists — are driven out of their lands in North Carolina, and join this "Iroquois Confederacy" in the early 1700s. And it's still with us, in the form of the Six Nations Reserve by Ontario's Grand River — where there grows a great swamp elm. The people themselves call it *Kaya-nerenh-kowa* ("The Great Peace") or *Kanonsionni* ("The Longhouse"), which is both the kind of dwelling in which the Iroquois once lived, and the kind of parliament or congress that administers the law.

... BUT I WOULDN'T WANT TO LIVE THERE!

Coquitlam, B.C., from Salish: stinking with fish slime

Cultus Lake, B.C., from Chinook: worthless, foul, anything bad

Slocan, B.C., from Okanagan: pierce in the head

Komoka, Ontario, from Ojibwa: quiet place of the dead

Les-Méchins, Québec, French, from Mi'kmaq *matsi*: evil monster

Cape Maringouin, N.B., French: point of land full of mosquitoes

Metchosin, B.C., from Salish: oil of a dead beached whale

Pikangikum, Ontario, from Ojibwa: dirty water narrows

Puvirnituk, Québec, from Inuit: it smells of rotting meat

Quaqtaq, Québec, from Inuit: intestinal worms

Horsefly, B.C., from English: horsefly

Kejimkujik Lake, N.S., from a Mi'kmaq word for a body part that can't be mentioned in polite society

FIRSTS FROM THE FIRST FOLKS

Did you know that the First Folks invented . . .

the canoe

snow goggles

the kayak

the toboggan

the dogsled

the travois

snowshoes

popcorn

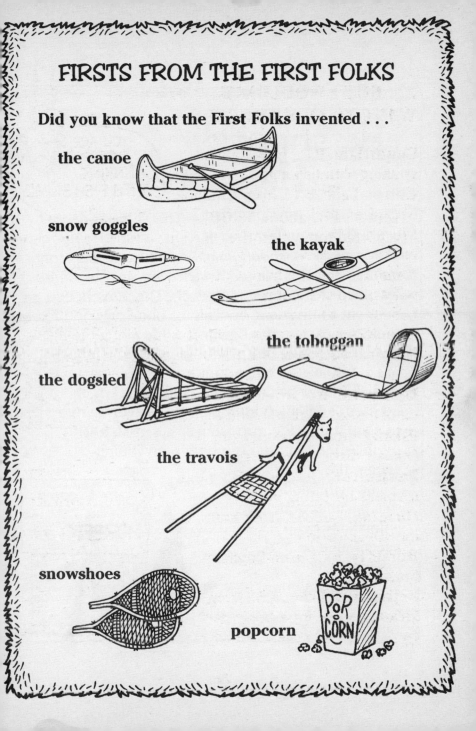

He shoots!
He scores!

Down east, about 1500 — The Mi'kmaq reported today that they have developed a winter game called "*oochamkunutk*" — which is easy for *them* to say. It is played on a frozen river or pond, with two sides of ten men each. The players use deer gut to tie runners of sharp bone or wood to their moccasins, the better to slide along the ice. Two goals, made of upright sticks or small heaps of stones, are set a few hundred paces apart.

Each player has a curved stick, with which he tries to hit a wooden ball, the object being to send it into the opposing side's goal. It is permissible to hit an opponent anywhere except the head.

The likelihood of this peculiar activity enjoying wide acceptance or popularity is exceedingly slim.

GAMES PEOPLE PLAY

Do you play lacrosse? If so, tip your hat to the First Folks. They started it centuries ago.

But they didn't call it "lacrosse." French priests gave it that name because the shape of the stick resembled a bishop's crozier or cross. It was about a metre long, with a net pouch at one end, and it was regarded as an object of great value. Some men (no women allowed) were actually buried with their lacrosse sticks. (No, not when they were still alive!) The ball, about the size of an orange, was made of wood, or of deerskin stuffed with hair. The Algonquin called the game *baggataway*, from the Cree word *pakahatuweo*, "he plays ball." And it wasn't just a sport or a game: it was also a healing ritual for somebody sick, a way to settle an argument between clans, and a deadly serious rehearsal for war.

Here are some instructions for a typical lacrosse game of 400 years ago:

1. Pick a playing field about a mile or more long — for us, that means about a kilometre and a half. Don't worry about the width. There are no sidelines. Place the goal posts at each end.

2. Train for weeks by running, jumping, wrestling, praying.

3. Don't eat too much, especially the flesh of timid animals like the rabbit.

4. Don't eat at all the day before the game.

5. Don't touch a baby — its bones break easily and yours might, too.

6. The night before the game, dress up in your party clothes. Dance for an hour, jump in the river, dance for an hour, jump in the river, and keep on doing that until it's close to dawn.

7. Go to the shaman — he's sort of like the coach or umpire for this game — who will:
(a) ask the spirits to help you win, and confuse your enemies
(b) outline the game strategy and
(c) cut your arms and legs until blood flows. (Yikes!)

8. Join your teammates — about a hundred of them, or maybe a thousand — and strip down to your loincloth. Paint your body with ferocious colours. Stick a few feathers in your hair so you'll be as speedy and sharp-eyed as a bird.

9. Wait till all the bets are made — and hope your dad didn't bet your baby brother, or worse, your favourite horse.

10. Run screaming onto the field.

11. Play ball! The game itself was like a riot. There were only a few rules: each side had the same number of players, you couldn't touch the ball with your hands, and you weren't supposed to kill anybody on purpose. Bruises, cuts, bloody noses, broken arms and legs, fist fights, kicking, tripping — all were part of the game. And it went on for hours, sometimes days. Then the white guys came along and made a hundred more rules — most of them boring.

ᴛHE SAGUᴇ

"Just Watcʜ

TRADE FAIR AT TO'RON

Ice on the Great River of Kanata and the large waters to the west has now disappeared. It's time to get ready for the spring meeting at To'ron'to. Members of tribes near and far will come to barter and trade. The *Signal* has learned that goods of many kinds and from many places are expected. High-ticket items are copper ornaments, needles and spearpoints from the Michilimackinac; prized obsidian arrowheads from our Wyoming prairie brothers; and shells of wondrous size and shape from the shores beyond the mouth of the Great River. To'ron'to in the springtime — brisk bargaining, friendly feasts, good-natured games, splendid storytelling! Be sure to stop by our *wiki'wan*, located beside the three birch trees by the bay. Every tenth visitor wins a valuable prize! You may be the lucky one!

Mississauga Chiefs Hold Powwow

Chiefs of the Pigeon, Fox and Snake clans met in council two moons ago, to settle a hunting dispute, the theft of two canoes, and the return of the Pigeon chief's runaway daughter. All was resolved with courtesy, though the chief's daughter remains sulky.

Sap Stream Superb; Syrup Supply Soars

The Ottawa report that their maple festival was a huge success, with the trees running swift as a waterfall. All tribe members danced the dance of joyful praise at the end of the affair, which lasted seven suns.

NAY SIGNAL
Our Smoke!"

'TO TOPS IN TERRITORY

Wanted: Youth to train as shaman apprentice. Preference given to those with knowledge of herbs, animals, dreams. Willing to fast and be silent for long periods. Interviews at Cave of the Bear, any time. No triflers please.

Lost: Amulet, polished squirrel skull, magical properties, sentimental value. If found, return to *The Saguenay Signal.*

SPORTS
Final Round in Baggataway Playoffs!
Teams: Clan Beaver vs. Clan Eagle, best-of-three.
Place: where the river narrows.
Time: sunrise after the night of no moon.
Betting now open, oddsmakers favour Eagles 3-1. Pre-game wrestling matches, prizes. Post-game party, P.Y.O.P. (Pack Your Own Pemmican).

Old Medicine Woman Speaks
Asquutasquash or winter squash is good in many ways. If the pulp is mashed and spread on burns, it helps in healing. Wrapped in leaves and placed on the brow, it cures headache. The seeds of one squash, eaten raw, rid the belly of worms.

JELLIED MOOSE NOSE

1. Find moose.
2. Shoot moose (except in Newfoundland, where you just run over it with your car).
3. Remove nose of moose.
4. Do whatever you want with remainder of moose.
5. Boil nose for 45 minutes.
6. Remove nose and chill.
7. Pull out all hairs from nose.
8. Place nose in pot and cover with water.
9. Add: 1 sliced onion, 1 garlic clove, 1 tbsp. mixed pickling spices, 1 tsp. salt, 1/2 tsp. pepper, 1/4 cup vinegar.
10. Bring to boil, reduce heat and simmer until tender. Cool overnight in liquid.
11. Take meat from broth; remove any bony bits. You will have two kinds of meat: white from bulb of nose, dark from near bones.
12. Slice meat thinly, put in loaf pan.
13. Reheat broth to boiling, pour over meat.
14. Cool until broth has turned to jelly.
15. Slice.
16. Eat at your own peril.

Recipe from *Northern Cookery*, published by the Department of Indian Affairs (with a few extra instructions thrown in).

VIKING
VOYAGES

About a thousand years ago, Leif Ericsson (or Leifr Eiriksson, take your pick) set foot (or feet) on North America. He was the first European to do so. Some people claim that Irish explorers (including a monk named Brendan who really got around), landed in Newfoundland in the sixth century and on Cape Breton around 875. But there's no proof. (Just as well: we could be living in a place called O'Hoolihan. Or Murphy.)

Back to Leif. He was the son of Eric (or Eirik) — which you probably already figured out, duh! — Thorvaldsson. Eric was kind of a gangster: he was thrown out of Norway because he murdered somebody (a popular Viking hobby), so he went to Iceland. Leif was born there about 970. Or maybe 975. A few years later Leif's daddy got into trouble again, fighting and messing around, and he was thrown out of Iceland. What a guy! He was rapidly running out of countries — at least, ones with names. So he set sail westward and bumped into a place he called Greenland. Now Greenland, as we know, is not noticeably green, but Eric wanted to promote tourism: he figured more people would come and settle in something called Greenland, rather than something called Ice-Rock-and-Not-One-Tree-to-Be-Seen-Land. ◄

The scam worked. By 985 there were a couple of settlements, and more folks on the way. One of them was a trader, Bjarni Herjolfsson, but he got blown way off course and ended up near the coast of good old North America, probably Labrador and Baffin Island.

He finally made it back to Greenland and told everybody about "a level land covered with woods." This is where it gets unfair. Hardly *anyone* has ever heard of Bjarni Herjolfsson. *Everybody* has heard of Leif Ericsson. But without Bjarni, Leif would be left out of history. Anyway, Leif listened

---

This is a good story but it may not be true. History is like that. On some ancient maps there's a big island in the northern ocean named *Cronos*, or *Cronland* or *Groenland*. Perhaps Eric, in between murders and fights, saw one of these maps and thought the hunk of ice he'd run into was this island. Nobody knows.

to the stories and got hot to trot. When he was twenty-four or so — a tall, blond, blue-eyed, handsome dude with great abs and pecs — he bought Bjarni's boat, gathered up some of his buddies and shoved off. His dad would have gone too, but he was thrown from his horse that morning and figured it was a bad omen. What a guy! (A note about the boat: this may be disappointing, but experts are pretty sure it wasn't one of those wicked-looking Viking jobs, sleek and skinny and fast, with pointy ends and a dragon at the prow. It was probably a *knarr*, a merchant boat, round-bottomed and wide and slow, to carry cows and groceries and beer and people. Think minivan, not muscle car.)

So one day in the summer of 995 (or 1001, take your pick), after a quick look at Baffin Island (which they called *Helluland*: "land of flat rocks") and Labrador (*Markland*: "land of thick forests"),

Leif and his friends jumped overboard and splashed ashore at a place they called Vinland. Leif's foster father, Tyrkyr, found some grape vines there — get it, Vineland?

Where is Vinland? Nobody really knows for sure. Could be Newfoundland, could be Cape Cod, could be West Palm Beach. But it was a heck of a lot warmer than Greenland, so they stayed the winter. Then they loaded up the *knarr* (or the Leif-boat, heh-heh) with timber, and went back home. Leif took over his dad's job as the big enchilada, or maybe the big herring, in Greenland, and died in 1018 or thereabouts. The family tree was Leif-less.

Hel and other destinations

Leif went to *Helluland*, but not to *Hel*. He became a Christian as a young man — and converted his mother, too, who thereupon began to give his father the cold shoulder, not to mention arm, knee, foot, etc. Dad went looking for company elsewhere, thereby adding to his sins.

Hel, or *Niflheim*, was the Norse land of the dead, with nine levels. The first level, which was gloomy, cold and boring, was reserved for those who died peacefully. The ninth level was definitely *not* boring. It was awash in the venom of a thousand thousand

GREAT PARTY FOR A BUNCH OF DEAD GUYS!

serpents which endlessly tormented all murderers (like Leif's dad), adulterers (like Leif's dad), and perjurers (probably like Leif's dad). Just to add to the fun, a giant dragon slowly sucked the blood from their bodies.

On the other hand, if you were killed in battle, it was party to the max, dude! You were instantly beamed up to Valhalla, the hall of slain warriors, to be with the head god, Odin, and await *Ragnarok*, the final rumble between the gods (good) and the giants (bad). To pass the time, you feasted on roast pig and chug-a-lugged liquor from a weird goat. And you fought all day, every day, hacking off a leg here, an arm there, a head elsewhere.

The next day all the bloody body parts were miraculously reattached — to the right stumps, too — so you could start fighting again. (Curious note: to fire up their ferocity, the warriors ate a certain mind-altering toadstool.)

PLAY BALL!

The Vikings played a special game on New Year's Eve, with 200 players or more. The aim was to get a ball from one end of a narrow street to the other. So what's the big deal about that? The Vikings used the severed head of an enemy for the ball.

THE BRATTA

Today: Cold, windy, snow
Tomorrow: Colder, windier, snowier
The day after that: Fuhgeddaboutit!

Greenland's Groo

THORVALD ERICSSON DIES
IN SAVAGE BATTLE

Thorvald, brother of Leif and son of the late Eric, succumbed to wounds inflicted by ugly, hairy, dirty, nasty savages in the new lands. While exploring the coast of Vinland, Thorvald and his crew came upon nine creatures asleep under what seemed to be boats made of animal skin. "They weren't human," said crew member Ranulf Ranulfssen, scratching his misshapen nose and shaking his tangled mane out of his eyes. "They looked like *skraelings*." *[Ed. note: readers will remember the ancient stories of* skraelings, *or trolls, hiding in the forest, which once frightened children.]* This sentiment was echoed by first mate Olav Olavssen, who said, "They weren't human. They looked like *skraelings*." He spat on the ground and wiped his nose with his sleeve as Ranulf Ranulfssen added, "So we killed them." Olav Olavssen agreed, saying, "So we killed them." However, one creature unfortunately escaped and ran off into the woods. The following day, as the crew boarded their ship, a host of *skraelings* appeared in their strange skin boats. They let loose a blizzard of arrows, and one of them found its mark. Ranulfssen said,

HILD *B*ANNER

*N*iest Gossip Gazette

WE CUT A LONG STORY SHORT
Oktober 26, 1005

"Thorvald was mortally wounded." So did Olavssen. Thorvald is buried on a grassy cape in the new lands, facing the sea he loved. *Farvel og skaal, bror!*

BIRTH NOTICE

Karlsefni/Thorbjorndottir — Thorfinn and Gudrid are delighted to announce the arrival of their son Snorri, born in early winter 1009 or possibly 1010, in a hut built by his Uncle Leif, somewhere on the Atlantic coast of the new-found land. The darling little pillager is welcomed by all. Especially remembered at this time are Grandfather Eric in *Hel*, and several uncles who died violently and continue to do so. Thanks to Aunt Freydis for her strong hands; and to second cousin Bjornstjerne for the lovely loot-bag.

For Sale: Used Irish thrall, male, 12 years, reasonable. Orm Svensson, Kirkegard Fjord.

Will trade horsemeat, near-fresh, for good milk-cow. Asa Bjornisdottir, Sikkerhavn Ost.

Rune-carving for fun and profit! Arne Johannessen, Skjonnstrandhus, nummer 7.

Freydis the Fierce

The other Ericsson kids were hooked on adventure, too. A year or two after Thorvald was killed, Freydis got the itch to travel. She was Leif's half-sister. Her first trip to the new world was with Thorfinn Karlsefni and his wife Gudrid, Leif's widowed sister-in-law, along with 250 others. They landed at *Leifsbudir*, a bunch of huts built by Leif a couple of years earlier, and settled in, along with some cows and sheep and goats. It was a terrible winter. They caught only a few halibut, the hunting was lousy, and fodder for the animals was worse than scarce. They stole eggs from seabirds' nests. They ate part of a whale rotting on the beach . . . then upchucked most of it. The brightest event of the season was the birth of Snorri, the first European child born in North America.

In the spring they split and sailed farther down the coast, making camp by a sheltered bay. There, two weeks later, they were visited by natives in kayaks, who were each given a drink of milk from a Norse cow and some strips of red cloth, and went away happy. Okay so far.

But the following spring a huge gang of *skraelings* showed up, looking for another slug of milk and more red cloth. Everything was peaceful as they landed, but suddenly Karlsefni's bull rushed out of the woods, roaring like a . . . well, like a bull. (Must've been that red cloth.) This scared the heck out of the natives and they took off.

But they came back — and they were really cranky. The Norsemen got into battle mode in a hurry, with red shields up and swords unsheathed. A storm of arrows flew, but that wasn't all. The *skraelings* launched their secret weapon, later described in the Norse sagas as "a pole with a huge knob on the end, black in colour, about the size of a sheep's belly, which flew over the heads of the men and made a frightening noise when it fell." The natives didn't have any sheep, so it was probably a blown-up moose bladder. And we all know there's nothing scarier than a blown-up moose bladder, right? The Norsemen panicked and ran off in all directions.

Freydis was really ticked off. She yelled at the men, called them a bunch of wimpy microbes, but that didn't slow them down. Finally, disgusted, she ripped off the top of her dress, slapped her naked chest with a sword and let go with a shriek right out of Friday the 13th. And we all know there's nothing scarier than a shrieking, chest-beating woman, right? (Unless

41

it's a blown-up moose bladder.)
The natives stopped, looked,
listened — and bolted for their
boats.

But the Norse hope of a
permanent settlement was down
the tubes. With the locals pelting
them with various unpleasant
objects all the time, life would
be too hard, not to mention too
short. So they loaded up the
ship and sailed north, stopping at
one point to murder five sleeping
natives out of sheer meanness.

Is Freydis discouraged? No way.
In 1013 or so, she's ready
to try again. And on this voyage,
she makes her father Eric look
like a pussycat. This is one tough
babe — she could fill a morgue
before breakfast! You think Lady
Macbeth was bad, with those
dinky little drops of blood on her
hand? Hah! Before Freydis was
done she was hip-deep in gore.
Want to hear about it? Thought
so. It's a tricky plot, so listen up.

1. Freydis outfits her own ship, with
a little help from her Ericsson kin.

2. She sets up a deal with a pair of Icelandic brothers, Helgi and Finnbogi. They have a ship, too.

3. Here's the plan: the two ships, each with twenty-five men and a few women, would sail to the new lands, load up the boats with good timber, then sail home and split the profits. Simple, straightforward, fair.

4. They reach *Leifsbudir*, and right away there's trouble. Freydis takes over Leif's big house and won't let the Icelanders inside the door. They have to build their own place, and they get pretty grouchy about it.

5. Things go downhill fast. Finally the two groups don't even speak to one another.

6. Freydis decides she wants the Icelanders' boat. Why not? It's bigger than hers. So she tells her husband, Thorvard, that Helgi and Finnbogi have been flirting with her all the time. At first he pays no attention but she keeps needling him, teasing him, mocking his manliness.

7. Thorvard loses it. He rounds up his crew and they attack the Icelanders. They slaughter all the men.

8. Not to be outdone, Freydis slaughters all the women.

9. She gets the ship, stashes all their stuff, abandons her own ship and goes home, swearing the crew to secrecy.

10. She tells the folks in Greenland that the other group wanted to stay behind for the winter, but one of her crew blabs.

11. Leif tortures three sailors until he gets the truth.

12. He can't do much about it, because Freydis is family, but he does put a curse on her children. All of them grow up to be first-class losers.

That marked the end of any real attempts at colonization by the Greenlanders. They made trips to get wood — Newfoundland was a lot closer than Norway — but they didn't stay. In time, even the Greenland colony died out.

Score one for the *skraelings*!

L'ANSE AUX MEADOWS

On the tip of Newfoundland's Great North Peninsula there's a little bay called L'Anse aux Meadows. In the land near that bay, evidence of a Norse camp — talked of for centuries, scoffed at for centuries — was finally uncovered in 1960. The Norwegian husband-and-wife team of Helge (writer, explorer) and Anne (archeologist) Ingstad dug up the proof, thus demonstrating the truth of the old adage, "You can lead a Norse to water, and he'll find a missing link." Here are a few of the unburied treasures: the remains of three houses, with workshops attached; a blacksmith's forge (the first in North America); needlework tools, and pieces of spindles and knitting implements — which means

the Norse brought their wives along (real Vikings don't knit) and meant to hang around for a while; and a bronze pin. Science has now shown that all this stuff dates back to the years between 950 and 1050, just about the time that Bjarni and Leif and Thorvald and Gudrid and Freydis — and the unfortunate Icelanders — might have voyaged through the stormy Atlantic, to stand on the shore of the new-found land.

At L'Anse aux Meadows there's no meadow in sight. *Anse* is French for "small bay or cove," but where does "Meadows" come from? From the jellyfish in the bay, of course. Experts think that "meadows" is just a lousy pronunciation of the French word *méduse*, which means "jellyfish." A jellyfish, with its many waving tentacles, looks like the fearful Medusa of Greek myth, who had snakes instead of hair, and who turned men, women and possibly sheep, stone cold dead without batting an eye. (Sounds a bit like Freydis.) So our Viking camp is really — Jellyfish Cove.

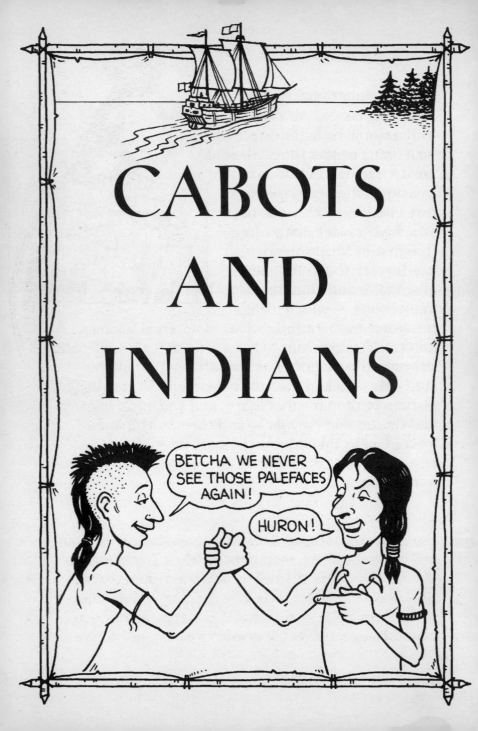

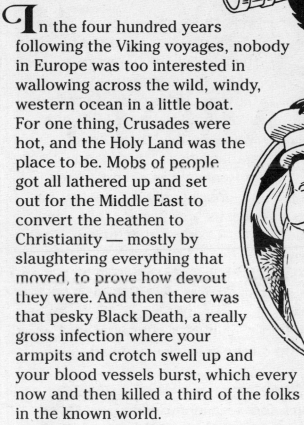

In the four hundred years
following the Viking voyages, nobody
in Europe was too interested in
wallowing across the wild, windy,
western ocean in a little boat.
For one thing, Crusades were
hot, and the Holy Land was the
place to be. Mobs of people
got all lathered up and set
out for the Middle East to
convert the heathen to
Christianity — mostly by
slaughtering everything that
moved, to prove how devout
they were. And then there was
that pesky Black Death, a really
gross infection where your
armpits and crotch swell up and
your blood vessels burst, which every
now and then killed a third of the folks
in the known world.

But then the price of pepper, cloves and nutmeg
went sky-high, thanks to greedy merchants who
controlled the supply. This was serious stuff. Without
any refrigeration to keep meat cold, or any spices to
shovel onto it, meat smelled bad and tasted worse.
Beef was often alarmingly green. Eating a pork chop
was a heroic act. And mutton? Forget it, unless you
fancied maggots. People needed spices. And where

47

were those spices? China, mostly, so people once again started to think about going west to get east.

One of those people was Giovanni Caboto. We don't know a lot about his early life, but he was described by an Italian ambassador at the London court of Henry VII as a "very good mariner, of a fine mind, greatly skilled in navigation." (*Caboto*, by the way, means "coaster," or "one who trades along the coast" — bet you didn't know that). He needed a royal backer, so first he tried Spain. After all, Columbus had hit the jackpot there. No luck — or *nada*, as they say in Spain. Next he tried Portugal. Zero — or *zero*, as they say in Portugal. Then a light went on. England just might be the answer: the Brits were the last stop on the spice line and had to pay top dollar. Or pound.

So Giovanni, the sly dog, translated his name into English — John Cabot — and moved to Bristol with his wife and three sons, Louis, Sebastian and Santius. Then it was off to London to visit the King, Henry VII.

Now Henry was still kicking himself for turning down Columbus a few years earlier, and was only too ready to support John's scheme, especially since John said he'd put up the cash. In the spring of 1496, John got the go-ahead: the King had granted permission to "our well beloved John Gabote, citizen of Venice, and to Lewes, Sebastian, and Santius, sonnes of the said John . . . full and free authoritie, leave, and power, to sayle to all partes, countreys, and seas, of the East, of the West, and of the North, under our banners and ensignes, with five ships . . . and as many mariners or men as they will have with them on the saide ships, upon their own proper costes and charges, to seeke out, discover, and finde, whatsoever iles, countreyes, regions or provinces . . . whatsoever they bee . . . " Whew! Are you still with me? That's the way they talked back then. That's the way they spelled, too — any way they wanted to.

John couldn't afford five ships. He got one instead, the *Mathew*, and a cute little thing it was. You could've put it in your school swimming pool. It could carry only 50 tuns. No, that's *not* spelled wrong: that's how they used to measure ships. A tun is a huge barrel that holds 252 gallons of wine. So the *Mathew* could transport — let me see now — 252 x 50 is — um, er, well, a heck of a lot of wine. But it didn't. They needed room for John, Sebastian and seventeen sailors. Oh, and John's Italian barber.

Log of the *Mathew*, John Cabot, Master

20 May, year of Our Lord 1497 — Left Bristol harbour at sunrise. Fair weather. River pilot Jas. Ray with us to Avonmouth, then put ashore. And now it's avast and belay there, me hearties.
(Must practise my sailor talk.)

22 May — Ship quick and sea-friendly. Ireland to starboard this morning. Wind northeast. Had beard trimmed after bird got trapped.

31 May — New moon tonight in western sky. Hair in ears trimmed. Sebastian whining in cabin, asks, "Are we there yet?"

7 June — Wind due north; *Mathew* took it on her beam, soft as can be. Punished two crew after knife fight in rigging. Addlepates could have damaged the sails. Made them attend workshop on anger management, and repeat a hundred times, "I must not fight with my fellowes."

11 June — Crow's-nest person shouted "Land ho!" Stupid crow's-nest person. Was floating cliff of ice, big as Westminster Abbey! Hove to smartly, but 'twas a near thing. Nevertheless — my heart will go on. Sebastian set stockings on fire, stupid boy. Should have brought Louis.

17 June — High seas, heavy blow, northwesterly. We lay a-hull, with small stormsail set.

Tried pigtail, as homage to Oriental custom. Crew frightened — of weather, not pigtail.

Sebastian whining, asks, "Are we there yet?"

YOU HANDSOME DEVIL!

21 June — For 2 days and nights — but we cannot tell what is day and what is night — fog has surrounded us. We daren't move, imprisoned as we are in vast bubble of froth. Crew uneasy. We must press on. The truth is out there. Split ends a worry.

ABANDON SHIP!!

23 June — Sun shining. Birds flying. Fish jumping. Pine trees smelling. Land approaching. Nose hairs removed, not without pain.

24 June — St. John the Baptist Day, a good omen. And land is but two furlongs to port! Gave thanks to Our Lord. Told Sebastian we were "there." Combed hair, shaved. Soon, Cathay and the Great Khan!

ROUGH SEAS TODAY, EH CAP'N?

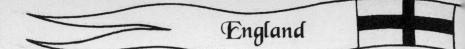

The land John saw was not the country of the Great Khan. It was most likely the northern tip of Newfoundland, very near the Viking settlement at L'Anse aux Meadows.

Hugging the coast, the crew travelled south, going ashore near what's now Griquet Harbour. Single-file they marched across the strand: the cabin boy, clutching a bishop's cross, John, Sebastian (probably still whining), a party of mariners and, of course, the barber. They

stopped in a clearing, and there John jammed two banners into the ground: St. George for England and the winged lion of St. Mark to honour Venice, his old home town. He took possession in the name of Henry VII — without even bothering to ask if maybe the place belonged to somebody else. He soon discovered that it did — to tornadoes of black flies, and mosquitoes as big as chickens. Then he saw a couple of fish nets and some snares and figured there might be human beings around, but he didn't actually see anybody.

Then it was back to the boat. He sailed down the coast until he reached Placentia Bay. Placentia Bay is deep. Like, DEEP. John kept slinging his 100-fathom rope overboard, but he never hit bottom. The bay was unfathomable, heh-heh. "Yippee!" he exclaimed. "I have found the passage to Cathay!" Not. Nor did he find any pepper, nutmeg or cloves. What he found was — cod.

Much, much cod. So much they just about jumped into his boat to get away from the crowd. So he zipped along home — making it in fifteen days — and told everybody. The cat was out of the bag, or the fish out of the sea. Whatever. King Henry was happy — after all, this meant England: (1) owned what Cabot had discovered, and (2) didn't have to depend on Iceland for fish. Henry gave £10 "to hym that founde the new Isle."

The following year Cabot set out again — without Sebastian — with five ships and a year's supplies, to found a colony. He never came back.

This doesn't sound like much. Nowadays it would be about $22, but in 1497 it was a lot. John's house rent was only £2 a year!

CRABBY CHRONOLOGY II

1350 Bubonic plague (the Black Death) kills a third of the people in Europe. The rest just hunker down and pray a lot.

c. 1350 Natives in lower Great Lakes region begin to cultivate beans.

1360 Expedition from Norway, with priests aboard, sets out for Greenland to make sure everybody's going to church, misses Greenland altogether, heads into Hudson Bay, James Bay, the Albany River, and ends up at Lake Nipigon. Major oops.

1381 Wat Tyler leads Peasants' Revolt in England, protesting forced labour and low wages.

c. 1400 Thule people spread eastward into Labrador. (*Thule*, or *Thyla*, ancient Greek name given to unknown northernmost land, supposedly "six days saillinge out of Bretayne.")

1450 Johann Gutenberg builds a printing press with movable type, even though the Chinese had already done it in 704.

c. 1450+ Huron villages grow bigger and more complicated, from a dozen or so longhouses and a few hundred people to forty longhouses and a few thousand people.

1453 The Turks take over Constantinople, pick off stray Christians from the west trying to get to China. **Powerful city-state** of Venice corners the market on spices, hikes prices. (Europe needs spices to make rotting meat edible — even approachable!) Again, people ponder going west to China via a shorter northern route.

c. 1475 Maliseet — who played a kind of football with wild abandon — and Passamaquoddy people leave permanent coastal villages, move inland, for reasons unknown. Maybe better football fields.

1492 A deluded Italian named Cristóbal Colón, a.k.a. Columbus, nags Spain's Queen Isabella, gets cash, sails to the Bahamas, thinks he's in India. He calls the natives Indians. Everybody still confused.

1497 Giovanni Caboto, under an assumed name (John Cabot), sails from Bristol, England, in a tiny ship. He lands in Newfoundland, thinks it's the tail end of China, claims it for England.

c. stands for *circa*, meaning "around, about"

1498 Cabot tries again, with five ships. One experiences technical difficulties, stops in Ireland. The others go on. They never come back. Cabot kaput.

1500 The Huron nation moves north to settle near Georgian Bay, trying to get away from hated Iroquois. It works for a while. Then it doesn't.

c. 1500 Sioux Assiniboine tribes move north from Minnesota into what's now Manitoba.

1501 Gaspar Côrte-Real, a pushy Portuguese and a pet of the king, sets out to win fame and fortune. Sails northwest with three ships, rediscovers Greenland, thinks it's Asia. Hoo boy! Blocked by ice, he turns south to Labrador and Newfoundland. Claims land for Portugal. Captures 57 Naskapi and Beothuk; they end up in Portugal as slaves. Gaspar's ship sinks. He's in it. Gaspar gasps his last gasp. Serves him right.

ASIA? WHAT DO THEY THINK THESE ARE, CHOPSTICKS?

c. 1520 The horse — ancestor of which had disappeared from the continent thousands of years earlier — is introduced by Spanish in the south, begins to appear in the north via intertribal trading (and raiding!). In two centuries it will change native way of life.

1524 Giovanni da Verrazzano, Florentine supersailor, explores Newfoundland coast, figures out that continent not joined to Asia or China. Duh. Kidnaps native boy, takes him to France. Later lands in Guadeloupe, is barbecued and eaten. Serves him right.

1528 Sebastian Cabot turns from whining to lying. After claiming in 1509 that he'd found the way to China (not true), he goes to South America to steal gold, but his men (a) mutiny or (b) are killed by natives. Another Cabot kaput. He drew pretty good maps, though.

1534 Jacques Cartier goes cruising up a river on a sunny afternoon, but thinks it's a bay. Looks around: no gold or jewels. Darn! Parties with Mi'kmaq and Iroquois. Meets Iroquois chief Donnacona, who invites him to visit "Ka-nah-ta," Donnacona's home. Cartier takes two of Donnacona's sons back to France.

1535 Jacques heads down river once again, says, *"Mon Dieu!* It is a river! *Un fleuve*, how you say, big time! *C'est la mère de tous les fleuves!"* He sails up and down for a while, visits village called Hochelaga, later named Montréal. Stays the winter. Bad move: cold, snow, scurvy, misery, death. In spring kidnaps Donnacona and ten others, including four children. Goes home. All kidnappees, except one small girl, die within a year.

1541 Jacques gives it another shot, this time to found a colony. As master pilot under bossman Sieur de Roberval, he sails ahead and winters near Stadacona (later called Québec City).

1542 La Rocque de Roberval, viceroy of Canada (Ka-nah-ta), arrives in Québec with a bunch of "colonists" (sprung from jail for the occasion). One is hanged for theft (first death penalty in Canada), another pardoned for murder (first document recorded in Canada).

1543 Roberval hangs a couple of dozen more for disobedience. Sixty die of cold and scurvy during the winter. Only a few left now, so he goes home.

1576–8 Martin Frobisher, once and future pirate, looks for gold and Northwest Passage to China. Finds neither, but thinks he's found both. Claims Greenland and Baffin Island for England. Takes three Inuit and 200 tons of iron ore back to London. Ore soon proves goldless. Inuit die.

1583 Humphrey Gilbert (half-brother of Walter Raleigh) explores Newfoundland, claims it for England, doesn't ask Beothuk if they mind. Rude. More flags stuck in this new-found-land than in your average golf course.

1585+ John Davis, a buddy of Gilbert and Raleigh, is obsessed with Northwest Passage, makes three trips, can't get through ice floes. Plays football with Inuit. Maps Greenland (which he calls "Land of Desolation"), Baffin Island and Labrador. Names a strait after himself.

1603 A couple of big-shot fur traders sail for Québec and Samuel Champlain goes along for the ride. They land at Tadoussac, where naked Algonquin women dance for them. Champlain figures the place deserves a closer look.

Why Red Skins?

Native North Americans were often called "redskins," "red men" or "red Indians." (The words are still around, as in the Washington Redskins football team.) Why? There's a story that John Cabot saw a few Beothuk in Newfoundland whose bodies were daubed with red stuff, whereupon he went home and said, "I saw some redskins!" Balderdash and poppycock. John didn't see a soul. But later explorers certainly did. What they didn't realize was that the red stuff was ochre,  and the Beothuks plastered it on so the mosquitoes wouldn't bite them. The skeeters bit the white guys instead.

RED
OCHRE

NO
RED
OCHRE

So what's ochre? Well, it's a type of earth consisting of a mixture of hydrated oxide of iron with varying proportions of clay in a state of impalpable subdivision. Now you know.

¿QUICKIE QUIZ?

1. Every now and then John Cabot shouted the command: "Cast the lead!" What did he want his men to do?
(a) put on a play
(b) make some bullets
(c) get the lead out (move faster)
(d) measure the depth of the water

2. What is a fathom?
(a) a really big bottle of champagne
(b) a puzzle
(c) 6 feet (about 2 metres)
(d) a hug

3. What is a furlong?
(a) the pole you wrap a flag around
(b) the length of a furrow on your average cornfield
(c) the hide of a very tall weasel
(d) a word you use when you're asked to look after your snotty little cousin, as in, "Not furlong!"

1. (d) To measure the depth of the water, sailors threw a strong rope, with a lead weight attached to its end, over the side of the ship. The rope, or cable, was usually 600 feet (100 fathoms) long.
2. (c), but also (d). A fathom was the distance between the outstretched arms of the average sailor, about 6 feet (1.8 metres). But the word itself comes from the Old English word *faethm*, "the embracing arms." — a hug.
3. (b) "Furlong" was originally "a furrow long," the length of one side of a 10-acre square on a medieval English farm, about 220 yards (201 metres).

JACQUES
THE SKIPPER

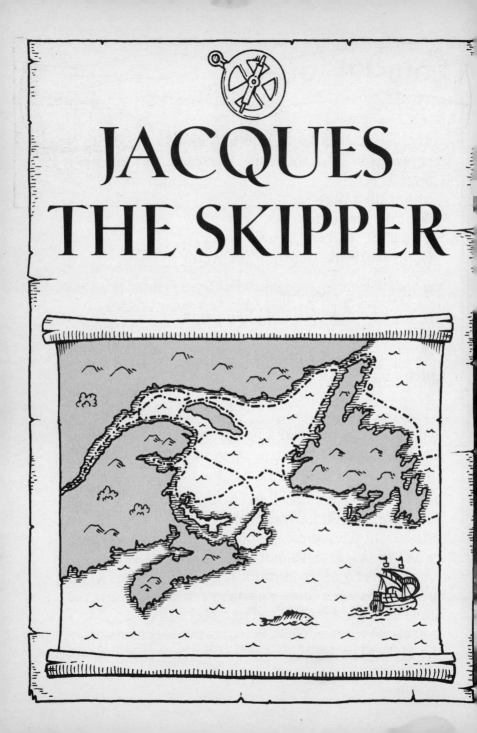

The First Voyage

In 1532, François I, King of France, made a pilgrimage to Mont-St-Michel, the spectacular abbey on a rock near the coast of Brittany, where the tide roars in like a runaway train. The poor fellow probably needed divine help — he'd had a run of bad luck you wouldn't believe. He lost a war and half his kingdom to Spain and Germany; he spent ten months in a Madrid prison; his wife died at age twenty-four after giving birth to seven kids in seven years (no wonder — she needed the rest); his mother died of the plague; two sons, aged seven and eight, were held hostage by Spain for four years; his eldest daughter died; he caught syphilis; and he had really bad headaches.

Anyway, while he was there, François and the boss of the abbey, a big-shot bishop named Jean Le Veneur de Tilliers, got together for a business lunch (omelette, croissants, a good if somewhat pretentious red wine) and did a few deals. François suggested that maybe the bishop could keep the crackpots from burning too many Protestants at the stake. The bishop wondered if François might consider sending a sailor from St-Malo, who happened to be a cousin of the church treasurer, to the new lands across the ocean.

Nods and smiles all around, with a little ring-kissing on the side. Of such is history made.

The sailor from St-Malo ◄ was Jacques Cartier, the second of the three big Cs — Cabot, Cartier, Champlain — in the story of the country he would soon name. (Also a big C. *Hmmm.*)

Cartier, then forty-one years old and a master mariner and pilot, already had a lot of miles on him. He'd been to South America more than once, and knew well the Grand Banks and the east coast of Newfoundland. Two years later, events unfolded as arranged. With a budget of 6000 *livres* (a whacking big lot of cash), Jacques outfitted two ships, signed up 61 men, bought some groceries, and on April 20, 1534, set out "to make the voyage from this kingdom to Terres Neufves, to discover certain isles and countries where there is said to be a vast quantity of gold and other rich things." In other words — "Hey guys! Let's go rob the natives blind!"

On May 10 (depending on your calendar), Skipper Jacques sighted Cape Bonavista, Newfoundland. Icebergs barred his way ashore, so he sailed 15 miles (24 kilometres) southeast to Catalina.

Cartier's home town was originally named St MacLaw or Maclou after a monk/disciple of St. Brendan the Navigator, he who held Mass on top of a whale. (On his way, possibly, to Canada. *Hmmm.*)

There the men sewed sails and mended masts for ten days, while a west wind blew most of the ice out to sea. Then they went northeast 80 miles (128 kilometres) to an island full of great auks, murres and gannets, which, Cartier reported, "bite even like dogs." They shot birds until their arms were tired, ate a few for supper, and stuffed twelve huge barrels with the rest. In an astounding burst of banality, Jacques named the place *Île des Oiseaux*. Later, after somebody took a few deep breaths, the name was changed to Puanto — or "Stinking" — Island. Now it's called Funk.

Sailing northwest to Cape Bauld, right at the tip of Newfoundland, they marvelled at a swimming polar bear, "as big as a cow and white as a swan." Marvellous it might have been, but they murdered it anyway. Then they ate it, finding "its flesh was as good and delicate to eat as that of a two-year-old steer."

On they went, nosing into coves, circling islands and islets, crossing bays and baylets, zigging,

zagging, exploring the coast of Newfoundland and Labrador, eating whatever they could find, with Jacques the Skipper drawing maps and making notes all the way. He didn't think much of Labrador. As his report to the King stated: " . . . this . . . should not be called Terre Neuve, being composed of stones and frightful rocks and uneven places; for on this entire northern coast I saw not one cartload of earth . . . there is nothing but moss and stunted shrubs. To conclude, I am inclined to regard this land as the one God gave to Cain." (This did not stop Cartier from planting a flag and claiming the land for France.)

Turning south again, Cartier spotted some natives paddling along the shore, likely Beothuk hunting seals. He said of them: "The men are well enough formed but untamed and savage. They wear their hair on top of their heads like a fistful of twisted hay, sticking into it a pin . . . and . . . some bird feathers. . . . They paint themselves with tan colours . . . " The crew didn't shoot them — surprise, surprise. Might have been the only living things they skipped.

Cartier poked about on the west coast of Newfoundland, filling in the blanks on the map, stopping for a day at a tiny island so the crew could kill a thousand gannets just for the heck of it. Then it was off to what we know as Prince Edward Island. Jacques never discovered that it was an island, but in his view it sure beat Labrador as a vacation spot. On June 29 he wrote: "this land . . . is the fairest one could see . . . " The crew often went ashore " . . . to see the trees, which are marvellously beautiful and sweet-smelling . . . cedar, yew, pine, white elm, ash, willow . . . " The meadows were "very fair and full of pease, white and red gooseberries, strawberries, raspberries, and wild wheat . . . and there are many turtledoves, wood-pigeons, and other birds." (Which they undoubtedly shot.)

Jacques still wanted to get to China, though, so he sailed north to a bay so warm he named it *Chaleur*. Here he met Mi'kmaq in canoes waving furs at him. Swap time! The French forked over knives and spoons, and a red cap for the chief. The Mi'kmaq happily gave up their old clothes. News of the trade got out, and two days later 300 Mi'kmaq showed up, bearing gifts of broiled seal flipper. (Don't knock it till you've tried it.) Cartier's men responded with hatchets and rosaries. In return the women ran to the crew, rubbed the men's arms as a friendly gesture, stripped off the furs they were wearing — took the hides from their hides, so to speak — and sold them on the spot. Cartier's men responded with applause. There are no further details of this encounter. Just as well.

Then it was anchors aweigh again, although the skipper had a little trouble getting all the men back on board, and off to Gaspé Bay — the most important stop on the journey, as history was to prove. For here it was that Cartier met the native chief Donnacona and 200 of his people. They had come from their village of Stadacona (later Québec) on a summer fishing trip for mackerel. And also to have a look at the odd-looking white men, dressed in odd-looking clothes, living in odd-looking canoes, of whom they'd already heard. Jacques thought the natives were just as odd-looking. He noted that their only garments were loincloths as small as G-strings, and fur

scarves. Their heads, he said, were shaved "except for a topknot that they leave as long as a horse's tail, which they bind and tie to their heads . . . with strips of leather." He figured they were flat broke and had no fixed address, not realizing they were just on a fishing trip and travelling light.

Both groups knew how to have a good time,

though. On July 22 all the sailors left their ships and joined the natives for a beach party. They danced and sang and ate together, and Jacques gave a little bell to each of the three young women at the festivities. Pleased, the girls did the usual ritual massage.

Suddenly two dozen more girls (who had wisely been hidden by the men of the tribe) rushed from the forest to surround Cartier. They all wanted bells, and were ready to rub to get them. They got them. (Why Cartier travelled with so many of the little tin bells remains one of the mysteries of history. Back in Europe, they were used by falconers to keep tabs on their birds. But Cartier seems to have *shot* birds versus keeping tabs on them . . . so why the bells?)

The party went on and on and everybody was happy, but only for two days. On July 24 Jacques spoiled the mood. He put up a huge 30-foot (almost 10-metre) cross, uttered reverent exclamations . . . and all the French fell to their knees and prayed. Talk about your party poopers!

Donnacona didn't understand the words, but the minute he saw that cross go up he got the message: That hairy paleface with the fancy hat was staking a claim and trying to swipe his country. (He was dead right, too.) So he put on his best black bearskin, went to the skipper and told him, in eloquent and unmistakable sign language, to get off his property. Wily Jacques calmed him down and showered him with gifts, saying he didn't mean any such thing. He lied. But Donnacona trusted him, so much so that he let Cartier take two of his teenaged sons, Domagaya and Taignoagny (easy for *him* to say!), back to France. Cartier left the next day, with a promise to return the following year.

Donnacona, who treated all guests with friendly courtesy, assumed Cartier would do the same, would follow the Golden Rule and "do unto others as he would be done by." But Jacques — never a big fan of Matthew 7:12 — had his own golden rule: "Do unto others as much as you can, and the gold will pile up nicely, *ka-ching, ka-ching*!"

Lemon-Aid

Your gums swell up. Then they bleed. Your teeth get loose and wobble around in your mouth. Then bruises pop up all over your body. You feel lousy. You don't want to eat much, partly because three of your teeth fell out yesterday. You get a cold. And then another. You're weaker than an overcooked noodle. Your get-up-and-go gets up and goes. Then the skin on your legs splits open in big, ugly, raw, wet sores. All your bones hurt like mad. You are one sick puppy. Congratulations! You've got scurvy! Why? Because you haven't been eating your fruits and veggies. You are nutritionally challenged. Serves you right.

Scurvy (from Old English *sceorfian*, "to scrape," and *sceorfan*, "to gnaw or bite"; and Old Norse *skurfur*, "scabs") was the scourge of old-time sailors. They'd be at sea for weeks and months and never eat fresh vegetables or fruits, which are loaded with vitamin C. They ate salt pork and hardtack, a biscuit that tastes like old newspapers. One lemon, one lime, one orange, or even a cup of raw turnip a day — anything with vitamin C — and they would have stayed healthy. And yet the connection between what people ate and what disease they got wasn't made (by any European) until 1753 when James Lind, a Scottish naval surgeon, figured it out. But the First Folks had known the cure for centuries.

The Name Game

When Domagaya told Jacques Cartier that he had reached the land of *kanata*, the Skipper heard the word as "Canada," and assumed it was the name of the whole country. There's strong evidence that it meant only "village," or "group of huts," or "Hey look! It's the boys in the 'hood!" Or maybe even, "Let's send out for double-cheese pizza." Whatever.

From then on, the word and the land were one. Not that everybody thought it was a good idea. During the 1860s, when union with the Atlantic provinces was brewing, dozens of new names were suggested, some of them obviously by guys who weren't the sharpest knives in the drawer. For example:

Acadia: from *Archadia*, name given by Verrazzano to Atlantic area in 1524, itself from Greek *Arcadia*, a paradise of trees and grass and sheep and nymphs, bossed by god Pan

Albertland or **Albertoria:** to honour Queen Victoria's husband, Prince Albert, who died in 1861

Albionaria or **New Albion:** *Albion* is an ancient name for Britain

Albona: who knows?

Alexandrina: to honour Queen Victoria, her first name being Alexandrina

Aquilonia: from Latin *aquilonius*, northerly

Borealis : from Latin *boreas*, the north wind

Cabotia: to honour the vanished Giovanni

Canadensia: Latinized version of Canada

Champlain: after Samuel Champlain, of course, a.k.a. Sam the Tripper

Colonia: from "colony" (Let's hope so, anyway!)

Hochelaga: native village, site of what later became Montréal

Laurentia: for the St. Lawrence River, itself named for the patron saint of the poor, who was roasted on Emperor Valerian's outdoor grill in A.D. 258, and whose last words were reported to be: "Turn me over, please. That side is quite done."

Mcsopelagia: Greek for "land between oceans"

Superior: Latin for "upper," "higher," "greater"

Transatlantica: beyond or across the Atlantic Ocean

Transylvania: *Yesss!* And our national emblem would be a bat! Too bad the name — which just means "beyond the forest" — was already taken

Ursalia: from Latin *Ursa Major*, Great Bear — the land under the Great Bear or Big Dipper, a constellation in the northern sky

Vesperia: from Latin *vesper* for "evening, evening star;" hence, land of the sunset

And how about this pair of acronyms:

Efisga for England, France, Ireland, Scotland, Germany, Aboriginal

Tupona for The United Provinces of North America.

We stand on guard for . . . Mesopelagia? Efisga? I don't think so.

IT'S ABOUT TIME

In Cartier's time, the world moved a little bit slower. Or so folks thought. When Julius Caesar wanted one sensible calendar instead of the crazy six or seven then in use, his clever Egyptian astronomer, Sosigenes, made a tiny mistake. He figured a year was exactly 365.25 days long. It isn't. It's 365.24199 days. He was off by 11 minutes and 14 seconds. So, over time (ho-ho), time got out of whack. By 1542, it was 10 days out of whack. Forty years later, Pope Gregory XIII finally fixed it, mostly so that the Christian Easter would fall where it was supposed to, on the first Sunday after the first full moon after the spring equinox (March 21).

The solution? First, Gregory lopped 10 days off the calendar and announced, "October 5 is now October 15." Second, he said, "Every four years we'll add a day, except in century years unless you can divide them by 400, like 1600 and 2000." Got that? Presto! The Gregorian calendar, now used by most Western countries, was born.

PLEASE, NOT MY BIRTHDAY!

75

The Second Voyage

Cartier got high fives all around when he reached St-Malo with Domagaya and Taignoagny. The whole town turned out to cheer and clap and gawk at *les jeunes sauvages*. It was a zoo. Think big rock star. Jacques was so pumped he bought a little farm and ordered a coat of arms for himself. Once upon a time you had to be a king or a duke to get a coat of arms, but by 1500 anybody with loot could own one. By the way, you can still visit his farm — it's near the tiny village of Limoelieu, just outside St-Malo. And on the stone entrance gate you'll see his coat of arms, with its anchor and cross rampant — on a field of dead auks. (Just kidding.)

In a year or so Cartier was ready for another try, this time with 110 men, and three ships on loan from the French navy: *La Grande Hermine*, the 120-tun flagship, *La Petite Hermine*, 60 tuns, and the 40-tun *L'Émerillon* — or, *The Big Weasel, The Little Weasel* and *The Sparrowhawk*. (The weasel, or ermine, was important in Cartier country. It appeared in the coat of arms of Anne of Brittany, married to François I's dad, King Louis XII — who was something of a big weasel himself, losing three wars and wearing out three wives.) Jacques's orders were: explore beyond Newfoundland, discover faraway countries, don't kidnap anybody and don't mess around in every little bay and village on the way. Like, hit the road, Jacques!

They sailed out of the harbour on May 19, 1535. With Cartier, as promised, were Donnacona's sons, eager to go home. The young men had learned two things: the French language, and the French plot to take over their country. (Plus a third thing: real braves don't eat quiche.)

Fifty days later, on July 7, after scary storms and vicious west winds, *The Big Weasel* sighted Funk, a.k.a. Stinking Island, a.k.a. *Île des Oiseaux*. Guess what they did.

Right. Got off the boat and murdered birds. (No wonder the great auk was extinct by 1844!) By late August they'd reached what's now Sept-Îles, where the kids got all excited and told Cartier that this was *le chemin du Canada*. Jacques got all excited too, now sure he'd found the way to Cathay. When they reached the Saguenay River, the boys spouted some wonderful lies about the "Kingdom of Saguenay," where gold and silver and jewels were all over the place and everybody was rich. Jacques tried to take the big ship upstream, but it was tricky navigation, with cliffs and rocks and rapids and enormous overhanging spruce trees, so he gave it up. They watched beluga whales and crowds of snapping turtles as they passed Murray Bay, and arrived at Stadacona on September 7.

Cartier wrote in his journal: "This marks the beginning of the land and province of Canada." The next day Donnacona came aboard, hugged his sons and kissed Jacques's bare arms. Everybody scarfed down bread and wine. Jollity ensued. They anchored at the mouth of the St. Charles River and had a party, with dancing and singing in the shallows, and much giving of gifts.

For a day or two it was a regular love-in. Then Cartier said he wanted to go up to Hochelaga. Oh boy. Stadacona and Hochelaga didn't like each other much — sort of like cats and dogs. And Donnacona thought he had the inside track with the French guys and all their neat stuff — guns, iron tools and extremely large canoes — and he didn't want to share. He felt as if the tipi trash down the road were out

to get his winning lottery ticket. The scene went like this:

Donnacona says to Jacques, "No way."

Jacques says, "Way."

Donnacona: "Don't go."

Jacques: "Sorry, chief, a man's gotta do what a man's gotta do. I'm goin'."

D. says, "I won't let the boys go with you to show the way."

J. says, "Who needs 'em? I'll go by myself. So there!"

Then Donnacona makes a big long speech about how good his folks are and how bad the Hochelagan folks are. He offers Cartier three children, as a sign of good faith and to cement the alliance with the Europeans.

Cartier says, "Are you out of your tree, Donnacona? I can't be bribed! But thanks for the kids."

It's a stand-off. The next day Donnacona plays his ace — a magic show. Three medicine men with

blackened faces, wearing dog-skins, and with long horns stuck in their hair, paddle out to the ship and go into their routine — a shouting match about as loud and long as the death scene in an opera. Then Domagaya and Taignoagny come aboard to play the king, queen and jack. They yell: "Our god predicts lousy weather, lots of ice and snow, and death on the river!"

Cartier just laughs and says, "Well, *my* God tells me the weather will be perfect. And a man's gotta do what a man's gotta do, or, *Un homme doit faire ce qu'un homme doit faire.*"

So Jacques, leaving some crew members behind to build a fort, took *The Sparrowhawk* and manoeuvred upriver, stopping at an island to eat boiled muskrat with five native hunters, and to add another young girl to his maiden collection. After that the river began to break up into little streams and islets, so they piled into the longboats and rowed the rest of the way, reaching Hochelaga on October 2.

Well! What a turnout! It was standing room only

on the beach, with a thousand natives shouting *aguyase! aguyase!* ("welcome! welcome!") and pelting the longboats with cornbread. The children were pushed to the front for Cartier to touch, and then they had an all-night rave — singing, dancing, setting fires, eating cornbread and yelling *aguyase!* with their mouths full. The next day Jacques got all duded up in his best dress uniform, called for his trumpeters, and with an honour guard of twenty sailors carrying pikes, marched to the Hochelagan headquarters at the foot of a great hill — which he promptly named Mont-Royal.

Here's the program for the day:

1. They go to an open space in the centre and sit down on bark mats. The women rub and stroke the sailors' arms. The sailors don't put up much of a fight.

2. Ten braves tote the chief in on a deerskin litter. He's paralyzed from the waist down, about fifty years old, and wears a red headband of porcupine quills. ("Porcupine" is from two Latin words meaning "spiny pig." Bet you didn't know that.)

3. Jacques rubs the chief's arms and legs, and gets the headband as a reward.

4. The sick, the blind and the lame appear. Jacques is told to lay his hands on them. He does. Nothing happens.

5. Jacques figures he'd better play along, so he slowly makes the sign of the cross, and then reads from chapters 18 and 19 of the Gospel of St. John — the gory details about the crucifixion. The natives don't understand word one, but they think it sounds great.

6. Cartier tosses handfuls of pewter (i.e., cheap) rings in the air. The children run around and pick them up.

7. The trumpeters blast out a few riffs. At first the natives jump about waist high in the air, but they love it.

8. Storytime: the Hochelagans tell Cartier more fibs about the people of the Saguenay — they are wicked creatures with tons of weapons, but very rich, with huts full of silver and gold. Jacques tries not to drool.

The following day the French got back in their longboats — some carried piggyback by the natives — and rowed out to *The Sparrowhawk*, arriving a week later at Stadacona. They moved into the fort built by the men left behind. Cartier met Donnacona the next day. Donnacona figured he'd better not pull any more fancy tricks, and was all smiley and buddy-buddy. But just as a little message — one about as subtle as an AK-47 — he showed Cartier a couple of hundred scalps peeled off enemy heads.

It was now the middle of October, far too late to set out for France. Jacques wasn't upset about this — he thought a Canadian winter might be interesting. He was right. *Sacré bleu*, was he right! The fellows went about gathering winter fu-u-el, salted down lots of fish and deer and rabbits (and birds — gotta have some birds), filled up the chinks in the log walls, rolled in a few barrels of wine, and settled in.

Jacques, as usual, made notes:

✦ about the natives running around bare to the waist in way-below-zero weather

✦ about their heavy gambling habit, often losing everything (weapons, *wampum*, a wife or two, and every scrap of clothing)

✦ about tobacco (the first mention of the weed by a European — a couple of the sailors actually tried it, but quit after one drag, saying it burned like a mouthful of pepper)

✦ and about what poor old uptight Jacques saw as a shockingly carefree attitude toward *les liaisons* (that's a French word for a really heavy date).

COLD?...WHY WOULD I BE COLD?

Both *Weasel*s and *The Sparrowhawk* were frozen solid in the river from November, 1535, to mid-April, 1536. The ice was "four fathom deep." That's more than 7 metres. Along the shores there was well over a metre of snow. And none of it went away till spring. All the barrels of wine, cider and water froze. Ten centimetres of ice coated every surface of the ships, above and below decks. Like, *cold*, man!

Then — scurvy! Scurvy, the age-old scourge of sailors. Bleeding gums, mouth rot, loose teeth, lost teeth. Swollen legs, pain, swollen arms, pain, sores, pain, open running ulcers that would not heal and grew infected — and more and more pain. In the middle of February Cartier wrote: "Out of the 110 men . . . not ten were well enough to help the others, a thing pitiful to see." Jacques prayed round the clock, bargained with the Holy Mother, and asked for a miracle. Lo and behold, he got one!

It was Domagaya. He dropped in one day on a friendly visit, and revealed the secret. You must gather branches of *annedda* (white cedar), he told Cartier. Then you grind the bark with your hard stone, and boil it in water. You drink the liquid each day, and spread the dregs on your limbs and sores. Things, he said, go better with cedar juice, even though it tastes like the inside of my grandfather's moccasins.

Within three days, most of the sailors were better and on their feet. Another name for the white cedar

is *arbor vitae* (Latin for "tree of life"), and Cartier is
said to have coined the term. While the cure came
too late for twenty-five of his men, it saved the lives
of all the rest.

Now back to Donnacona. He loved tall tales, and
he didn't mind playing fast and loose with the facts,
as long as it made a good story. He told Cartier stuff
about Saguenay that was straight out of something
like *Gulliver's Travels*. He said he'd been there
himself and seen mountains of gold and hills of
rubies. He said all the people were white as snow

and clothed in fine wool. He said one country there was full of one-legged pygmies, and another was home to people who lived on liquids only, because their bodies didn't have rear exits. (Don't giggle. It's not funny: imagine a diet of Coke and chicken soup and cedar juice.)

Cartier believed every word. Which was too bad for Donnacona. Cartier was so knocked out he decided to kidnap Donnacona and take him to France so he could tell King Frank in person. On May 3 — the Feast of the Holy Cross, a day you'd expect good Catholics to be pure in word and deed (this is irony, by the way; look it up) — the sailors pounced on Donnacona, two of his sidekicks, and Domagaya and Taignaogny, and carried them off to the ship. Including the boys and girls he'd been given as presents, Cartier took ten natives back to St-Malo. The Stadaconans wept and wailed in anguish all night long, but Cartier didn't relent. He threw some trinkets at them, said he'd be back in a year, and sailed away on May 6.

At first, life in Paris was a big hoot for Donnacona. He told his stories (which got wilder and wilder), he was a big favourite at court, he ate well, he was baptized, he got a pension.

Then after four years of living it up, he got sick — probably with something as simple as a cold — and died. He was buried (nobody knows where) as a Christian. Domagaya and Taignaogny, his two sons, grew bored with court life and took off in search of adventure.

They vanished into the dangerous Paris underworld and weren't heard from again. One little girl survived — how, we don't know. All the others died, never again to breathe the beloved air of their home in "Kanata."

Your Account Is in Arrears

At Hochelaga, Cartier saw beads made from clamshells used as money. To guarantee a good supply, the natives slashed the thighs and buttocks of their dead enemies, and stuck the corpses in the shallows of the river. Clams would burrow into the cuts and cheekily make themselves at home. Result? An ATM for instant cash withdrawal.

The Third Voyage

Captivated by Donnacona's tales, King François merrily fractured the tenth commandment and began to covet his neighbour's everything. He figured the Saguenay was the plum in the pie, his ticket to the high life, the way to get in on the action, i.e., the rape and pillage of other countries. After all, that's what kings did, right? João III of Portugal was rolling in money from slaves and spices, and Charles V's Spanish "explorers" were busy ripping off Peru and Mexico of all things bright and beautiful, with a little mass murder here and there just for fun.

Donnacona's stories got spicier. The Saguenay, he claimed, had cloves, nutmeg and pepper; orchards full of oranges and pomegranates; and creatures who had wings instead of arms. When challenged, he put one hand on the white man's Bible, crossed the fingers of his other hand, and swore it was all true.

Well, King Frank could hardly wait to get going, and began to plan a third voyage — one with an army along, just like the Spanish and Portuguese.

This time, he told Cartier: Forget about China. Point your boat at Saguenay and go for the gold! It took a while because France and Spain decided to have a war for a few years. They did that a lot, mostly because Charles V wanted to be king of the world.

Jacques, who'd been given *The Big Weasel* by the king, passed the time by plundering the odd ship or three. Finally, on May 23, 1541, he was ready to shove off, with five ships and a couple of hundred "settlers" who were led onto the ships in chains. (Why chains? Because they were convicts. Nobody else would go: death by freezing, or scurvy, or a

sauvage in a temper tantrum, or boredom — or maybe all of the above — hardly guaranteed a bright future. More like no future at all.)

Most of the prisoners had been rounded up by Cartier's boss for this trip, a soldier of noble birth named Roberval, who never did much except execute people for being rude. On departure day, he was still scrambling around trying to get guns and ammunition (the better to execute people), and Jacques left without him.

So there they were on the ships: bandits and brawlers, con men and counterfeiters, forgers and firebugs, scammers and flimflammers, pickpockets and lockpickers, killers and kidnappers, thugs and thieves. Men, women and some children, too, were all crammed in with horses, goats, cows, pigs, chickens and sheep. Think about that for a minute, but try not to breathe deeply. At one point the water ran out (water ran out, heh-heh, get it?) and the goats and pigs had to drink hard cider. Now think about *that* for a minute: a bunch of billygoats

BIG WEASEL

and hogs reeling around the poopdeck half-snockered and listing to starboard. Does that sound like your average holiday cruise, or what? Three months later — it was a tough trip — they finally made it to Stadacona.

Agona, the new chief, and Jacques smiled and nodded and rubbed each other's arms. Agona gave Jacques a leather crown and two bracelets. Jacques gave Agona . . . the news of Donnacona's death. Agona had trouble keeping the grin off his face. Cartier then told outrageous lies about the other natives he'd taken to France, most of whom were dead or lost. He said they'd all married rich spouses, they were living as great nobles, and they were happier than a butcher's dog.

Still, just to be on the safe side, Cartier moved upriver about 9 miles (15 kilometres) to what's now Cap Rouge, unloaded the ships, and set the folks to building a fort and planting cabbage, lettuce and turnip. They also hammered away at rocks, filling two of the ships with "diamonds" and "gold," which Cartier sent back home on September 2 — to find out later that the "diamonds" were quartz and the "gold" was iron pyrite, laughably worthless stuff. (Which is how the expression *faux comme un diamant du Canada* entered French conversation.) In the middle of September he tried to sail up the Saguenay River again. No luck — he was rapidly routed. (Joke.)

Back to the fort. To stay the winter. Oh my. You'd think he'd learn. The men got scurvy again, but had enough sense to stew up some cedar. The natives, however, were restless. And suspicious. Definitely not their heretofore friendly selves. Jacques figured this out when several of his carpenters were killed while out fetching wood. Later the natives — who had at last realized that Cartier spoke with forked tongue, not to mention sword and gun and occasional crucifix — attacked the fort. Thirty-five palefaces were successfully transported to the happy hunting ground, some of them in bits and pieces.

Jacques packed it in. He'd had enough. His boss Roberval still hadn't shown up with the guns and bullets and troops, so Cartier broke camp in June and sailed for home.

And who does he bump into at Newfoundland? Roberval, who finally has his act together. They have a conversation, which goes something like this:

Roberval: "Where do you think you're going?"

Cartier: "Back to St-Malo, Your Idiotic Excellency."

Roberval: "No, you don't. You turn right around and come back with me."

Cartier: *"Va péter dans le trèfle!"* (Rough translation: "Go take a long walk off a short pier.") *"Un homme doit faire ce qu'un homme doit faire.* I'm going home."

And he did.

Roberval the Rotten

It's hard to talk about Jean-François de La Roque de Roberval without using words that make your mother clutch the sink. (And you know what they are, don't you?) He is one mean dude. Here's the skinny:

Born around 1500 into an ancient noble family — though the genetic fizz has gone flat by the time it reaches him — Roberval runs with the royals from an early age, hangs out at the court, and is really tight with King François. As a rare Protestant in a Catholic country, he skips the country for a while in the 1530s, to avoid a little torture session with the Inquisition. However, the King soon asks him back and puts him in charge of Cartier's third voyage. Nobody knows why exactly — Roberval has never commanded anything bigger than a duck in a bathtub — but being best buds with the King doesn't hurt. Anyhow, he jumps at the chance: he's flat broke and he owes big money all over France to loan sharks, and to dozens of cousins (once-, twice- and thrice-removed). He figures he and Jacques will hit the jackpot in the Saguenay. Along with founding a colony and building forts — and getting the gold in them thar hills — Roberval is supposed to put up some churches and convert the heathen to Catholicism. Just to get some practice, he turns Catholic himself.

In April of 1542, almost a year after Cartier sailed, Roberval is ready to go. Along with a few dozen convicts, ten or twelve playmates from the court go with him, thinking it might be a real blast. One of them is an eighteen-year-old cousin — to whom he likely owes money — named Marguerite de La Roque. (More about her later.) After a pleasant crossing, Roberval runs into Cartier at St. John's, Newfoundland, and orders him back to Canada. Jacques, fearing a mutiny by a crew who never want to see the New World again, blows him off and sneaks out of the harbour at midnight. Roberval throws a hissy fit, and flogs a convict or two to make himself feel better.

Then he finds out that his cousin Marguerite, with the help of her maid Damienne, had smuggled her lover aboard back in France. And that the pair of them have been tarrying under the tarp and frolicking in the forecastle all across the Atlantic. Well! The *ordure* hits the air-circulation device big time. Roberval freaks. He just loses it, and proceeds to demonstrate the true spirit of Christian compassion by abandoning Marguerite and her

maid on an island in the Gulf of St. Lawrence. Sweet guy, eh?

On they sail, reaching Cartier's fort at Cap Rouge at the end of July. It's too small, so they build a bigger one, with lookout towers, ovens, barracks, storehouses and an open square with a vegetable garden. Then Roberval goes off to find the Kingdom of Saguenay and gather up all the gold and silver and precious gems lying around. *Not!* He doesn't find the kingdom, doesn't find the loot and loses a longboat and the people in it trying to get through the rapids.

So it's back to the fort for the winter, and the real misery begins. The folks shiver, starve and go short on vitamin C. Yep — scurvy again. (The garden's a flop.) Sixty people die. The others want to go home. They whine a lot. Roberval gets out the whips and chains and nooses (or should that be neese?). Here's what André Thevet, a Franciscan monk and the first historian of New France, wrote: "Roberval was very cruel in dealing with his men, forcing them to work; otherwise they were deprived of food and drink. If anyone failed in his duty,

Roberval had him punished. One day he had six of them hanged and some he banished to an island in leg-irons, because of petty thefts of not more than five *sous* [about a nickel]. Others, both women and men, he had flogged . . . "

Sweet guy, eh?

Finally Roberval gives up, sends a ship back to France before the river ices up, and asks the King to come to his rescue. The King does so the following spring, and everyone who's still alive returns to France. So ends the colonial experiment. The scorecard reads as follows:

Forts built: 1

Towns built: 0

Churches built: 0

Treasures found: 0

Natives converted to the Holy Catholic faith: 0

Deaths by hanging, drowning, accident, scurvy, starving, abandonment, bad colds and excessive sensibility: about 100

Roberval is now bankrupt. He's being sued by everybody, all his property is mortgaged, and he's down to one *château*. He goes back to the Protestant church (after his short stint as a Catholic), which turns out to be his last stupid move. One night in 1560, leaving a Calvinist gathering in Paris, he walks smack into a religious riot and is stabbed to death in front of the Cemetery of the Innocents.

Sic transit Jean-François de La Roque de Roberval.

Marguerite the Magnificent or Cast Away

Remember Marguerite, the foxy cousin? Right. We last saw her on the shore of a little island in the Gulf of St. Lawrence watching the ship of her nasty relative, Roberval the Rotten, disappear upriver. (The island, called variously *Île des démons* and *Île de la demoiselle*, lies just west of the Strait of Belle Isle and offshore from Harrington Harbour, which you can find on a modern map of Québec.)

Beside her, wailing, is her maid Damienne, she who carried messages, arranged meetings, kept her mouth shut and generally acted the good and faithful servant while her mistress conducted a

shipboard romance. (With a fellow whose name we'll never know. Let's call him Brad. Or Leonardo. Or Joe Who. Or Whatsisname. Whatever.) Roberval has allowed them a few bits of food — he's all heart, isn't he? — and two harquebuses. (See footnote next page.) Suddenly they see something swimming towards them. *Qu'est-ce que c'est que ça?* It's a fish! It's a turtle! No! It's . . . Whatsisname! With a couple of guns and a bag of shot. Roberval forgot to throw Whatsisname in the brig and he jumped overboard. Ain't love grand?

And it is, for a few months. It's summertime and the livin' is easy. Fish are catchable, birds are shootable, bunnies are trappable. Whatsisname builds a cabin — clever lad — and the three of them play contentedly at *Survivor*. Then the north wind doth blow and so does, unfortunately, the snow. Whatsisname dies. Marguerite can't bury him because the ground is frozen, and she doesn't want the wolves to eat him. What to do? Keep him in the cabin till spring, of course. Without air freshener.

In April Marguerite has a baby. The baby dies. Now it's two against the wilderness. Somehow Marguerite and Damienne get through another winter. Then Damienne, loyal to the end, dies. Marguerite is alone.

Right about now those harquebuses 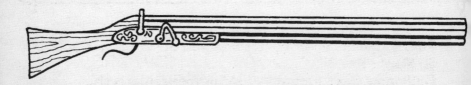 sure come in handy. Marguerite shoots duck and partridge to stock her pantry, and she kills a polar bear and two black bears that fancy a feast of fresh French female (or stale French male). Two-and-a-half years later, in the early spring of 1545, fishermen from Brittany who are trolling through the Gulf see smoke from her fire. They go ashore to find a skinny creature with tangled hair, and bones visible through her tattered clothes, who — *c'est si extraordinaire!* — speaks to them in their native language. Marguerite de La Roque is rescued and returns to France, where she gets some decent clothes, and becomes a teacher, a celebrity and the heroine of two books.

The harquebus or arquebus or hackbut was the first portable gun that could be fired from the shoulder. But it was often fired from a tripod-like support, which took the brunt of the recoil from a hook on the gun. Hence the name, which is from Middle Low German *hakenbuss*, "hooked gun." Bet you didn't know that. Bet you didn't even want to know that.

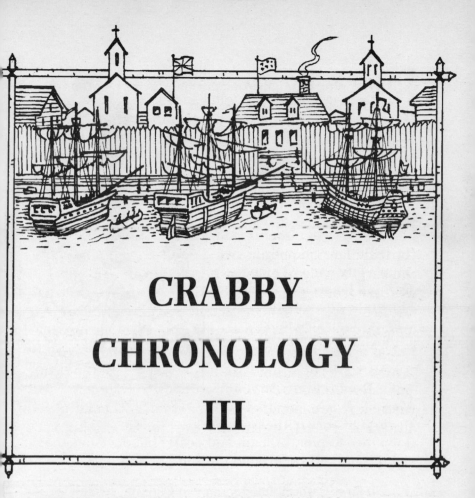

CRABBY

CHRONOLOGY

III

1604 Champlain discovers first iron ore in Canada at St. Mary's Bay, N.S.
Guillaume des Champs is first European to practise medicine in the New World. (He didn't practise enough — thirty-five people die of scurvy.)

1605 The French build a fort — without a windmill — at Port-Royal.

1606 Apples brought from Normandy are planted in Annapolis Valley. We now eat their descendants.

c. 1607 Six men in Acadia die from hard work, grinding grain by hand, after which (just a little late) a water-driven mill is built.
Europeans have their first cuppa tea, brought from Asia by the Dutch.

1608 Champlain begins to build a city named Québec.
German lensmaker Hans Lippershey invents the telescope. Galileo looks through it.

1609 Marc Lescarbot publishes *L'Histoire de la Nouvelle-France* in Paris, the first history of the New World.
Johannes Kepler, brilliant and nearly blind, claims that the planets revolve around the sun.

1611 First Catholic missionary in Canada, Jessé Fléché, teaches the catechism to Mi'kmaq chief Membertou and twenty family members in three weeks flat, then baptizes them.
Kepler (ever clever) explains the rainbow.
King James gets 54 highbrows together to rewrite the Bible. So far the Bible has sold more than 3,880,000,000 copies in 1,453 languages. (This book won't sell as many.)

1615 Father Joseph Le Caron celebrates the first Mass in Ontario, for Hurons near Penetanguishene.

1616 Priests start the first schools, in Tadoussac and Trois-Rivières. Your life has never been the same.

1617 Louis and Marie Hébert and their three children — the first European settlers — come, see, conquer the Québec wilderness, using only hand tools.

1621 Hatches, Matches and Dispatches (births, marriages, deaths) begin to be registered in Québec. (Canada is the only country with continuous birth records dating back more than 300 years.)

1622 Word has it that Étienne Brûlé discovers Lake Superior, even though it's been there for quite some time. Like, you know, a hundred centuries.

1625 Jesuit Jean de Brébeuf, founder of the Huron mission, martyr and patron saint of Canada, lands at Québec on June 19. He has 8,672 days to live.

1628 A first: on April 27 the land is "broken by the plough drawn by oxen," one year too late for hardworking Louis Hébert, who dies in 1627 after slipping on the ice.

1629 Champlain surrenders Québec to swashbuckling Englishman Sir David Kirke. The Kirkes sell Olivier, a black boy from Africa, as a slave to a turncoat French bookkeeper for 50 *écus*.

1632 France gets Québec back from England. **Franciscan priests** in La Have, N.S., build the first schoolhouse. Your life has never been the same. **William Oughtred**, Episcopalian minister and ace mathematician, invents the multiplication sign (x). Your life has never been the same.

1636 A foul-mouthed fellow in Québec is pilloried in the marketplace for swearing. **Giambattista Basile** of Naples writes the first version of *Sleeping Beauty*, in which a father accidentally eats his own children for lunch. An editor makes him revise it.

1638 On New Year's Eve a lunar eclipse scares the loincloths off the Huron. Some of them believe the Jesuit missionaries did it, and they get surly. Uh-oh.

1639 A number (a cloister? a flock?) of nuns arrive at the Habitation in Québec, ready to nurse, nourish and nudge the natives to salvation. **Hôtel-Dieu de Québec**, first hospital in Canada, opens. There's an immediate backlog in the ER.

1640 Somebody counts all the Europeans in New France. There are 375 of them. We don't know how many First Folks there were because nobody thought to count them. Duh . . .
Some Hurons catch Christianity but most of them catch smallpox. Half of them die.

1641 Brébeuf writes a Christmas song in the Huron language, "Jesus, He Is Born." It's known now as "The Huron Carol." Then he writes a description of Lake Erie, then called *Lac du Chat*. (*Erie* means "the place of the long-tailed one," that is, a panther, or wildcat.)

1642 Paul de Maisonneuve, Jeanne Mance and Marie-Madeleine de la Peltrie (who gives her heart to the Jesuits — after she's dead) get off the boat at Montréal Island and establish the town of Ville-Marie (Montréal). Paul's the governor, Jeanne's the head of the hospital and Marie-Madeleine's the local do-gooder. Their nineteen-year-old countryman, Blaise Pascal, a perfect nerd, invents the first digital calculator.

1644 Maisonneuve and thirty settlers defeat a band of Iroquois attacking Montréal. The natives blame whites for spread of famine and smallpox. They're right.

1646 After a fragile peace, Iroquois capture, torture and kill two Jesuits. Things are getting pretty scary, so the other priests decide to put on the first play in Québec, *Le Cid*, which is about a Spanish superhero who does all kinds of impossible stuff, then dies of grief because he lost a battle. Wimp.

1648 The Iroquois attack two Huron villages and kill everybody, including a priest. The first temperance meeting in North America is held at Québec on July 17 . . . and nine weeks later the first tavern opens for business.

1649 An army of Iroquois attack the Huron missions. They torture the priests, Brébeuf and Lalemant, for many hours. Many natives so admire Brébeuf's stoicism (look it up) under torture that they convert to his faith. **Oliver Cromwell** abolishes Christmas Day in England. **King Charles I** sticks his neck out for the last time.

1650 The Huron, what few remain, flee from their lands. Missionaries move out pretty fast, too. The French–Indian Wars have begun.

SAM
THE TRIPPER

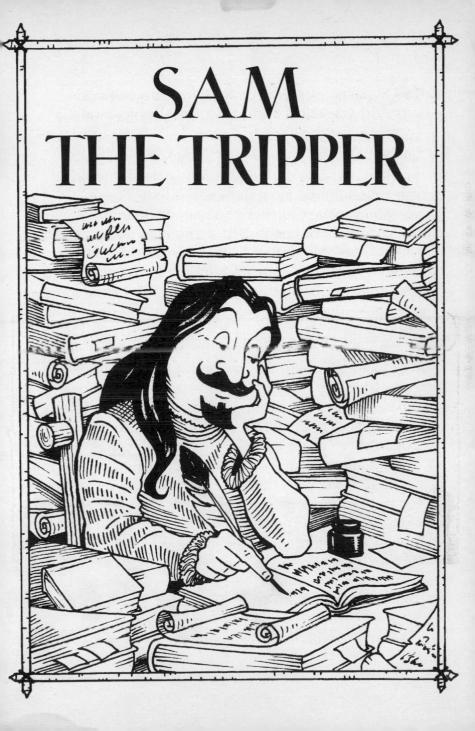

After the Cartier and Roberval disasters —
and half a dozen more — nobody in France much
wanted to cross the ocean and stay in a place one
writer called "a few acres of snow." But that big-
toothed, flat-tailed, tree-toppling, bark-munching,
stream-stopping, monogamous rodent, *Castor
canadensis*, the Canadian beaver, beckoned
irresistibly to anybody who wanted to make a few
bucks. For a handful of trinkets — a kettle, a knife,
a hatchet, a bell — the natives would deliver
gorgeous furs, which found a ready market and
fetched a handsome price in Europe. (So the white
guys cleaned up, but only for a while. The natives
— who'd been wheeling and dealing amongst
themselves all over the continent for centuries —
soon wised up and held out for better bargains.)

The French had set up shop — the first fortified
trading post in Canada — at Tadoussac in 1600.
There, three years later,
Champlain, who'd
hitched a ride with the
fur trader François Gravé
Du Pont, viewed the land
to which he would
devote his life.

He arrived on May 26,
1603, just in time for the
tabagies ("smokers'
meetings"), which is

SURE, ONE BEAVER PELT
FOR ONE KETTLE SOUNDS FAIR.

what the French called the feasts and round-the-clock partying staged by the natives, come to trade their piles of pelts. The men ran races and got a prize. The women danced naked and got applause. And smilin' Sam took notes, something he did every day of his life. He was a fanatic observer, full of curiosity, eager to learn and see and hear and marvel. And what he learned and saw and heard and marvelled at went into the many volumes of his *journals particuliers* — his diaries.

There's no room to relate all the daily details — of which Champlain was so fond — so we'll just hit the high spots. The low spots are sort of boring anyway. The heart does not beat faster upon reading stuff like: "Sailed to Canada, sailed back to France, sailed to Canada . . . " Or, "Brushed teeth with frayed elm twig, breathed in, looked at snow, breathed out . . . " Not the stuff of high drama. So, moving right along . . .

After the merriment and beaver swaps are over, Champlain rows up the Saguenay River for 12 leagues (about 58 kilometres). He's been told of a saltwater sea to the north, likely Hudson Bay. He doesn't reach it, but, in an astonishing leap of intuition, he surmises it's part of the Atlantic Ocean and not a route to China. (Yes, they were *still* on that kick!) Then he travels as far as Hochelaga, now empty, as is Stadacona, of the natives Cartier met. (Nobody knows where these folks went, but after being swindled by the slick and shifty sailor from St-Malo, they were wary of fellows with light skin. Some died of disease — which the Europeans gave away free — but most probably took off inland to live with other tribes.) Sam meets a group of Algonquin who tell him — via signs and sketches in the dirt — of the land that lies to the west. Champlain makes a remarkably accurate drawing of the Great Lakes and Niagara Falls, even though he's never been near them. Clever Sam!

Back he goes to Tadoussac, crosses over to the Gaspé and looks around. Likes what he sees. Gets a general idea of Acadia, thinks it's a better bet than the St. Lawrence area. In September he's in France telling Henri IV all about it: Acadia looks promising as a way to Asia and a source of metals and gems. Henri, who's just started a new love affair — of which he had too many to count — and can use some extra cash, listens and says, "Go for it, Sam!"

Champlain in Acadia

Sam goes for it. In the spring of 1604 he's just off the coast of Nova Scotia, this time with a fellow named Pierre du Gua de Monts, who not only is governor of Acadia but also has a ten-year monopoly on the fur trade in New France. They weigh anchor in a little bay. A sheep gets a whiff of fresh grass, jumps overboard and drowns, silly creature. The sheep (*mouton* in French) is instantly, if posthumously, famous: de Monts names the place *Port-au-mouton*; and on today's maps you can still find Port Mouton, pronounced locally as "Muh-toon," for reasons known only to Nova Scotians. (They haul the sheep back on board, by the way, and eat it.)

They follow the coast south and then north into the Bay of Fundy, amazed at the strength and size of the tide, the highest in the world.

Now and then Champlain goes ashore looking for mines and probable sites for settlement. Nothing

In Minas Basin, at the head of the bay, the difference between low and high tide is often 16 metres or more.

suits, but he makes wonderful maps.

In June the expedition crosses the Bay of Fundy. ("Fundy," from *Cap Fendu*, or Cape Split, the name of a long curly peninsula that splits the Minas Channel.) On an island near Passamaquoddy Bay in New Brunswick, Île Sainte-Croix, they build a palisade and a few small houses, and plant the first wheat in the New World. They decide to stay the winter — which turns out to be a really lousy idea.

It starts to snow on October 6. The snow doesn't melt till spring. It gets cold, then colder, then colder still. The food freezes. The water freezes. All the wine freezes. The men chop off chunks of it, and suck on wine popsicles. They should be sucking on lemons or cedar bark instead. Yep, it's scurvy time for the white guys . . . again . . . and there are no friendly natives around to smarten them up. By the time the snow vanishes there are only 42 survivors out of the original 77 men.

Not surprisingly, they vote themselves off the island. The following winter finds them across the Bay of Fundy at a place they call Port-Royal. It still exists. Today it's Annapolis Royal, and it's the earliest permanent settlement by Europeans north of Mexico.

Champlain builds a cabin for himself, diverts a nearby stream to make his own private trout pond, starts a garden and goes off looking for mines. Doesn't find any.

In the summer of 1606 a man arrives who will later be the first settler in Québec, the first farmer to make a living off his land, the first homeowner (his house was near rue Hébert in today's Québec City), and the first judge. His name is Louis Hébert. He's a skilled pharmacist and healer. He's a brave fighter, too, once splashing from ship to shore in his bare skin to save a couple of sailors from premature baldness through scalping.

NO DIAPER JOKES PLEASE.

Hébert may even be more deserving than Champlain of the title "Father of New France." By the time his daughter Guillemette dies in 1684, there are 250 Hébert descendants running around Québec. He left his name in Nova Scotia too (although they drop the accent there). Just south of the spot where that eager but unfortunate sheep jumped ship, you can visit Point Hebert,

Little Point Hebert and Louis Head.

Accompanying Louis is Marc Lescarbot, an all-round fellow who practises law, writes history books, devises dramas and composes really bad poetry. To him also belongs the honour of opening the first library in Canada. Most of his luggage is books, and he's quick to share them. In 1606 he writes, produces and directs Canada's first play, *Le Théâtre de Neptune*. (Halifax's Neptune Theatre, born in 1963, commemorates the event.) It's a real mish-mash, with folks singing the praises of the King and the Lord in three languages, cannons going off and trumpets blaring every now and then, while Neptune, clutching a trident, slowly drifts to shore in a canoe. The audience is appreciative but completely bewildered, especially the local natives. It closes after one performance.

COME ONE, COME ALL!
OPENING TONIGHT!

LE THÉÂTRE DE NEPTUNE

A Splendid Spectacle of Musical Drama
Written, Produced & Directed by The Renowned Lawyer,
Poet & Scholar M. MARC LESCARBOT

Recited & Sung in Three (3) Languages
(French, Gascon & Souriquois)

Starring Our Own **J. Cousteau** as Neptune, King of the Sea
and the **Brothers Mal-de-mer** as The Tritons
with **Painted Indians** as **Painted Indians**

Accompanied by Twenty Trumpets, Ten Drums,
Four Cannon & Assorted Harquebuses
Flowers: C. Baudelaire
Costumes: Y. St-Laurent
Candles: M. Tussaud
Refreshments: J. Valjean

Implements Supplied by:
Mi'kmaq Tool & Weapon Rent-All, the Straight Arrow Company
"If You Have to Axe, We Have the Answer"
"MORE BOW FOR YOUR DOUGH"

Audience is advised to stay seated
until all cannons have ceased firing.

The little settlement has a great winter. Only two or three snowfalls, mild temperatures, gentle winds, lots of food, much wine. Much, much wine. Sam, who is something of a party animal, founds *L'Ordre de Bon Temps* (The Order of Good Cheer, still cheerfully alive in Nova Scotia), whose guiding principle is "Let's get down, man!" Each member takes turns killing dinner, cooking dinner and entertaining the merry crew after dinner. Each member also vows to be in good spirits at all times. (What with the wine, it isn't hard.)

Because of some heavy-duty politicking in France, the fur monopoly changes hands in 1607, and everybody is ordered home. Sam goes the long way, sailing up the east coast of Nova Scotia, mapping every cape, cove, passage, point, inlet, islet, bay, beach, hill, harbour, nook and cranny he can find, and scattering French names with abandon. He reaches the eastern tip and calls it *Canseau* (now Canso), after the Mi'kmaq *kamsook*, which means "opposite the lofty cliff" (of Chedabucto Bay, Mi'kmaq *Sedabooktook*, "bay running far back"). He goes home with the first detailed map of the entire Atlantic seaboard from Cape Breton to Cape Cod.

Clever Sam!

COMMENT S'APPELLE-T-IL?

Why is this fellow's name sometimes Samuel de Champlain, and sometimes Samuel Champlain, without the "de"? "De" (of) — which in grammar is called a particle — usually means the person belongs to royalty or nobility. Like Helen of Troy, or William of Orange, or Anne of Cleves, or Emma Adelheid Wilhelmina Theresa of Waldeck-Pyrmont, or We Three Kings of Orient. (Just kidding.) The word after *de* is usually the name of a country or district or state or city. Champlain, however, is none of those: it's a combination of *champs* ("field") and *plain* ("level, flat").

So how come the *de*? After Champlain got famous, many people just assumed he was a high-born guy, and stuck the particle in between his first and last names. Sam didn't mind this a bit, so he wasn't in a big hurry to correct them. (Even though Sammy of the Flat Field doesn't make you want to genuflect, roll out the red carpet and fire a twenty-one-gun salute, does it?) But by the end of his life — one of great adventure and greater accomplishment — he deserved the *de*. He was *"un noble homme,"* indeed. There. That's settled.

Champlain at Quebec

*f*rance cools off on Acadia. The money from the fur trade, once expenses are paid, is pretty skimpy, and the Europeans decide to go back to the St. Lawrence region. Champlain, now lieutenant to de Monts, is at Québec on July 3, 1608. And before you can yell *T-i-m-b-e-r!* his men are felling trees, sawing planks, digging ditches and a cellar, and constructing three buildings, all surrounded by a 15-foot (4.5-metre) moat, and stockades of stakes.

Québec has begun.

After a tough winter in which two-thirds of the men, including a doctor, die of scurvy, and after hanging and beheading the would-be assassin Jean Duval (more on this guy later), Sam gets itchy feet. He's promised the Huron and Algonquin, his best buddies and beaver suppliers, that he'll fight the hated Iroquois. So off he goes, in late July, sailing up the Richelieu River with two countrymen and a bunch of natives, until he reaches a long skinny lake he names after himself. (No, it's not Lake Sam!)

They go ashore near what's now Ticonderoga ("between two waters" — Lake George and Lake Champlain) in *Iroquoia* (now known as New York state). On July 29 they meet a band of Iroquois.

It's showtime! Champlain steps forward with his trusty harquebus and blasts away. Two Iroquois chiefs drop dead. The others, panicked at the sound and fury of this weird metal stick, smartly take to the woods. This event does not make the Iroquois love the French; indeed, from that time forth they are sworn enemies. The Huron and Algonquin are delighted, of course, and they yelp with glee. Then they chop off the chiefs' heads and give one to Champlain as a trophy. Sam accepts with thanks. He's always wanted to get ahead.

The following year, after zipping over to France and back (ho-hum), Champlain fights the Iroquois again, near the same spot. This time he's wounded — an arrow nips his ear and sticks in his neck, but he just yanks it out, bleeds for a while, and goes on to win the fight. Brave Sam! However, this is the last time he beats the Iroquois. No more heads to hang over the fireplace. This year, too, he sends his young friend, eighteen-year-old Étienne Brûlé, off to live with the Huron and learn their language and customs. In exchange, the Huron ask Champlain to take one of their young men, Savignon, to Paris. Sam says okay and goes home to marry a twelve-year-old with money.

The next year Champlain's back in the new world (ho-ho-hum). So is Savignon, who struts around town telling outrageous tales about life in Paris. Sam takes a look at an island, Montréal, as a possible settlement, and — what else? — chops down a lot of trees. Then on June 13 he impresses the heck out of the natives by shooting the Lachine Rapids in a canoe. He's only the second paleface, after Brûlé, to do so. Brave Sam!

In 1613 he's finally recognized officially by the new king, three-year-old Louis XIII (because his mother Marie tells him to. Marie is Henri IV's widow. Poor Henri, who loved not wisely and far too often, was stabbed to death in 1610 by a Catholic with anger management issues and a very long knife.) Marie is a big fan of Champlain and makes him lieutenant to the viceroy of Canada, with all the powers of governor.

The next trip, later that year, is up the Ottawa River, the waterway that becomes the great trade route to the west. Champlain observes, maps, draws, makes notes all the way up to Allumette Lake, near Pembroke. He loses an astrolabe (an early navigation instrument — look it up) in nearby Green Lake and it's found 254 years later. He stops and talks to an Algonquin sub-tribe which takes its name from the lake. They discourage him from going farther, partly because the river gets life-threatening at that point, with stretches of wild white water, but mostly because they don't want to share Champlain with the Nipissing — their name means "sorcery" — who live to the northwest. Sam invites them down to Montréal, where they'd have better land and better protection from those nasty Iroquois.

They say sure, but only if Sam builds a fort. They know how to bargain. They know how to cut a good deal, too. Their chief, Tessouat, has a sweet little racket going, a kind of toll-road: Anybody going downriver past their camp must pay, in furs, or knives, or other worldly goods. Or sometimes people. No wonder they got on well with the French, because in Champlain's later notes he pushes for the same racket. (See Sam's blueprint, page 126.)

Got A Match?

Allumette Lake was named *Lac aux allumettes*, or "lake of matches," by early French explorers. *Allumette* means "little lighter," hence "match." But they didn't mean the kind of match we use today. (Those weren't invented until 1826, and even then it was an accident. John Walker, a druggist, was fooling around with a batch of chemicals, trying to make a new explosive. The end of his mixing stick got covered with the guck and he scraped it on the floor. *Whoosh*! John just about made an ash of himself!)

Before 1826, "matches" were usually skinny pieces of dry wood, which could be kindled with flint. Around Allumette Lake there are clumps of reeds — thin, strong, easily dried — and perfect for "matches."

By the way, you'd better think twice before asking someone for a match: the word comes from an old Greek term, meaning "burnt lampwick" or — Are you ready? — "mucus."

In 1615 Champlain is off again, with Brûlé, for Huron country. This time he gets past Allumette Lake to the Mattawa River (where you can find Champlain Provincial Park today), and follows the Mattawa to Lake Nipissing, a big shallow lake where the *doré* (for "golden," the yellowish colour of walleye or pickerel) are so abundant he can pluck them from the water with his hands. From there it's an easy route via the French River to Georgian Bay and Lake Huron, which is so big Champlain thinks it's a freshwater sea. He loves the country, with its fertile soil and magnificent trees (this is before people built Casino Rama, of course).

They hike down to Lake Simcoe, which won't be so named for 185 years, and meet with 500 Huron. They all get set to attack the Iroquois, urging Champlain to honour his many promises to help. Enough with the chit-chat, they say, now you gotta put up or shut up. Sam puts up — even though he thinks the timing is wrong, the battle plan flimsy and the outcome alarmingly iffy. But the natives have their best body paint on, and they're ready to rumble. Yippee! It's time for a massacre — followed by guaranteed hair removal.

Étienne Brûlé, with twelve Huron, goes ahead of the main force. His mission, which he chooses to accept: Ask the Susquehannah, allies who live south of the Iroquois, to join the fight. Brûlé's bunch paddles southwest on the Holland River to the

Upper Humber, where they're stopped by a
huge tangle of fallen trees and beaver dams. No
problem: they just put their canoes on their backs
and portage — for 28 miles (45 kilometres)! On
September 9, 1615, twenty-two-year-old Étienne
Brûlé, the first European to do so, stands on the
shore of Lake Ontario and the future
site of Toronto.

In the meantime Sam and the rest
of the war party cross Lake Ontario
around Kingston, hide their canoes,
and slog through the forest primeval
to a spot near Syracuse, New York.
It's now October 10. The trip has
taken forty-one days. And it's all for
nothing. The "surprise attack" is a
surprise only to the Huron because
the Iroquois are ready, waiting and
thirsty for enemy blood. What's
more, they're inside a fort with a
30-foot stockade around it. (That's
almost 10 metres to you — too

high to climb over.) The Huron are tired, cranky and can't get their act together. After a three-hour siege, they've had it. Sam takes two arrows in the same leg — one right in his kneecap — and is carried away in a big basket. And the Susquehannah, it turns out, have a curiously laid-back attitude towards time — they show up two days late.

Champlain really wants to go back to Québec — he's got a sore leg, and his normally high spirits have sagged a bit after the farce at Syracuse. But the Huron plead with him to spend the winter, and he gives in. It is then he records in meticulous detail, with the humane and respectful wonder that marks his character, the Huron habits, customs, diet, dwellings, dress (and undress) and their intense connection to the land. It's an EXTREMELY IMPORTANT document. But much as he asks, and asks, and asks again, about the country to the west, the Huron have little to offer. They're so busy building villages and planting corn and trapping beaver and hiding from the Iroquois, they never find the time to travel.

In May, 1616, Sam says farewell to the Huron, stops off in Québec to add extra rooms to the Habitation and pick up some wheat to show off in France, and heads for home. While he's been away, the usual political and corporate power plays have flourished, with bribes and double-crossing as routine as breathing. (*Plus ça change, plus c'est la même chose!*) Upshot: Champlain is downsized, de-hired, let go.

With time on his hands, Sam gets to know his wife a little better (after he remembers her name and address), and draws up an ambitious and masterful plan for the "civilization" of the New World. (Mind you, the folks who live in that "New World" aren't consulted, nor do they know they need "civilization." And it's not "new" to them — they've been living in it for 10,000 years!) Nevertheless, it's a great blueprint, a model policy for colonization, and a slick piece of PR, which Champlain presents to the King and the Chamber of Commerce in 1618. Here's part of it:

1. We can get to China and the East Indies via New France, "the short route." (Great balls of fire! Why don't they give this a rest?)

2. We can charge customs duty on everything that goes through Québec, west or east, and make a ton of money. (See Tessouat's scheme, on page 121.)

THOSE PALEFACES STOLE MY IDEA!

RIVER TOLL 2 FRANCS

3. France would own a huge country, "watered by the fairest rivers in the world."

4. We can save the souls of countless heathen savages.

5. We should found a city at Québec, with forts on either side of the St. Lawrence, and at Tadoussac.

6. For starters the town needs 15 priests, 300 families of four persons each, and 300 soldiers.

7. Someone from the King's council should be sent to establish a code of law.

8. Enormous wealth will come from "great and permanent trade" in: "fisheries of cod, salmon, sturgeon, eel, and herring; whale-oil and whale-wattles [yum-yum!]; timber of marvellous height; gum, ashes, tar; dye roots, hemp; mines of silver, iron and lead; coarse cloths, pelts, gems, vines, livestock." (Champlain has an eye to the future here, believing that a country can't survive on a single commodity . . . though Saudi Arabia seems to do okay. He's convinced the beaver hat is just a passing fad. He's right — won't our big-toothed buddy on the cover be glad to hear that!)

When Sam adds it up, the yearly take comes to about 5.5 million *livres*. In 1618 this is a *fortune*, and right away there's a whole lot of heavy breathing going on down at the Chamber of Commerce. King Louis, too, is gung-ho (from the Chinese *ganghe*, "work together") and says, "Sounds like a plan, man! Just do it."

Well, Sam tries to do it, and things look good for a while. King Louis gives him a pension of 600 *livres* a year, he collects the remaining 1500 *livres* of his wife Whatsername's dowry, and he crowbars a promise out of the businessmen — who suspect settlers might sooner harvest crops than beaver — that 80 settlers, with farm animals and seed, will go to Québec in the spring.

Over the next fifteen years, during which Sam sails back and forth half a dozen times, the little colony muddles along. It doesn't collapse, but it doesn't exactly prosper either. Champlain does his best to run the place — his life as an explorer is over — and keep everybody happy. It ain't easy. The settlers want more soldiers and forts. The priests (four of them come over in 1615) want a seminary for the natives, a ban on Protestants . . . and more priests. Champlain himself wants more settlers, more trade and more of everything except annoyances. And every now and then he goes out to the boonies (of which there is no shortage) and tries, with some success, to stop the natives from killing each other more than two or three times a week.

Sam is handy with a hammer, a skilled home fix-it fellow. In what little spare time he has, he fixes leaky roofs, shores up tumbledown walls, builds fences, paces off acres of gardens, and oversees the construction of a fort at Lachine, keeping his promise to the Huron. Shortly thereafter, a group of them come to Montréal, plant crops and settle in. Unlike many Europeans, both before and after him, Champlain never lies to the natives — at least the ones loyal to the French. His tongue remains unforked.

The conditions at Québec, never wonderful, grow worse after war breaks out between England and France in 1627. Supply ships from France are either late, or missing — many captured and plundered by the five Kirke brothers, who are authorized by England's Charles I 🦶 to take possession of Canada. To make the food go farther, Champlain sends some of the 150 settlers across the river to the Gaspé, to live off the land. It doesn't help. A grim situation gets grimmer. Now each person is allowed only seven ounces (about a handful) of dried peas a day. Mothers and fathers give up their portions to feed the kids. Then grimmer gets grimmest: they grind up what's left of the peas and make watery soup. This does not provide your recommended daily allowance of vitamins and minerals. *Au contraire.* Sam and his people are starving.

🦶 He was so bossy he later had his head chopped off.

On July 19, 1629, English ships appear offshore. It's the Kirke gang again. They've already captured Tadoussac and a couple of smaller forts along the river. They make an offer Champlain can't refuse: Hand over Québec or die of hunger. It's game over.

But not for long. Peace breaks out in 1632, England gives Québec back, and by the following May Sam's back in Canada, as busy as ever. He builds a chapel and a couple of forts, and rebuilds and enlarges Québec, which the English have totally wrecked. In 1634, still looking for the way to Cathay, he sends Jean Nicollet, a fur trader who has lived among the Allumette and Nipissing, to make contact with the natives west of Lake Michigan. Nicollet is so sure he'll find the route to China that

WHAT DO YOU SUPPOSE GOT INTO THEM?

he buys an expensive Chinese silk robe, gaudy with birds and flowers. He puts it on just before he meets the Winnebago ("people of the water smelling of dead fish") around Green Bay, Wisconsin.

Nicollet's the first white man they've ever seen, and he's quite a sight. They're terrified. They think he's a god come to punish them, and they hit the dirt, ready to tell him everything they know. (Which does not include the way to the China Sea. Too bad.)

Several dozen new French families arrive at Québec in 1634, and once more Sam, now over 65 but as optimistic as ever, has high hopes for his little colony. But in 1635 his health and strength, so remarkable all his life, begin to desert him. He makes out a will — which for some odd reason leaves all his furniture to the Virgin Mary even though She can't use it, with no mention at all of poor Whatsername. In October he has a major stroke which leaves him paralyzed. He dies on Christmas Day. He's first buried in an unmarked grave, then moved in 1636 to the chapel he himself had built. The chapel burns to the ground in 1640, and is later rebuilt, but after 1664 there's no mention of it at all. Sam's bones vanish.

But Sam doesn't. Champlain stands as a giant in Canada's history. Like Shakespeare's Julius Caesar, "he doth bestride the narrow world like a Colossus." Never discouraged, he was a risk-taker full of energy and vigour, with the immune system of Superman. At the same time he was a merry fellow, always ready with a joke or story, who formed deep friendships with the natives.

A superb geographer and mapmaker, and an observant and dedicated explorer, he unfailingly put his country first. Without him, New France — and Canada — could not have been born. *"Un noble homme," bien sûr!*

JUST A TRAVELLIN' MAN

Why is this chapter entitled Sam the Tripper? Because Sam couldn't sit still for ten minutes at a time, that's why. He was a travel junkie from boyhood on. Born around 1567 (nobody knows for sure because the parish church burnt down with all the birth certificates), he grew up in Brouage, a tiny town right on the edge of the Atlantic. The town's main moneymaker was getting the salt out of saltwater and then selling it to fishermen in the harbour, to preserve meat and fish. Champlain's dad sailed on one of those ships, and it wasn't long before the son followed in his father's footsteps, or deck shoes.

How far did he travel? Let's try to figure it out:

1. As a boy, fishing and fooling around along the coast of France: 500 miles
2. Trip to West Indies and back with uncle, around 1599: 10,000 miles
3. 1603–1633, 21 trips across the Atlantic, at 5000 miles each: 105,000 miles
4. Up, down, around, and through rivers, lakes, coasts, interior: 30,000 miles
TOTAL: 145,500 miles

145,500 miles! That's almost 233,000 kilometres! Which is like going around the world at the Equator six times. (And that's just the distance Sam's *boat* logged. We're not even counting him pacing the deck or walking to the privy.)

ᗩHE ᗧANADA ᗧHRONICLE

Bringing the World's News to the New World

July 15, 1608

Hot, humid
Black fly count: 1500 per cubic inch
Wind, SSW, 23 knots

DASTARDLY DECEIT DISCOVERED; PLOTTERS PUNISHED

L'Habitation, Québec — A shameful conspiracy to murder the respected Lieutenant Samuel de Champlain has now been revealed. A certain Jean Duval, locksmith, devised the contemptible plan in order to hand over the settlement at Québec to the Spaniards, in the hope of financial reward. He enlisted the services of four other scoundrels, including a certain Antoine Natel. It was Natel who had a change of heart — whether out of fear or remorse is not known — and informed on his fellow plotters. He has since been pardoned — a too-generous gesture, in our humble opinion.

All others have been tried and found guilty by Lieutenant Champlain and his ship's officers. With the exception of the villainous ringleader Duval, the criminals are en route to France where they are to be hanged by the neck until dead. Champlain ordered that Duval be hanged immediately, which just sentence was carried out two days past. He was then beheaded, whereupon the head was pierced with a pike and set atop the highest part of the fort, so that all can see and be warned of the wages of such iniquity. God be praised!

Snowshoes, all styles: Cree, Ojibwa, beavertail, swallowtail. Pre-season Sale! A. Dumas.

To Whom it May Concern: Please return the Holy Communion vessels to the chapel. No questions asked. No reward either. Fr. Robespierre.

Lost: Onondaga warclub, carved eagle grip, some stains. Keepsake. M. Chapdelaine.

THE SAILOR TIES THE KNOT

(The Double Hitch — followed by The Inside Clinch)

"Marry in haste; repent at leisure." So goes the old proverb, and Champlain must have taken it to heart. He didn't get around to it until he was forty-three. Of course, he was never in France long enough to hang out at the singles bars. But finally, on December 30, 1610, he married Hélène Boullé (or Boulay, or Boullay, or Boullet, or Boulé) in Paris.

Hélène was an upperclass kid, the daughter of the King's secretary. She was twelve years old at the time. If Sam were alive today and tried this stunt, he'd be thrown in the slammer. Back then it was okay, although the couple didn't live together until Hélène was fourteen, the age of consent. (Which is still pretty creepy.) You wonder why Champlain even bothered — but you stop wondering when you find out that Hélène brought some money with her, a dowry of 6000 *livres* (a *lot* of money back then), three-quarters of which went into Sam's pocket the day before he said, "I do."

In 1620, on her husband's ninth or tenth trip to Canada — it's easy to lose track — Hélène, now twenty-two, went with him. She stayed for four long years, and she was not a happy camper. Sam was running around being the Father of New France all the time, the log cabin wasn't a bit like the royal court, she didn't know any recipes for boiled squirrel or pike chowder (from the French *chaudière* for "big kitchen pot"; bet you didn't know that). And the weather was too cold, or too hot, or too windy, or too snowy, or too rainy, or just too weathery. Curiously enough, she got along beautifully with the natives, and they admired everything about her: her complexion, her hair, her gowns, her shoes —

and especially her little mirror, attached to the belt at her waist. (Mirrors were hot items, particularly in France. After somebody figured out how to make plate glass, around 1690, people bought mirrors instead of paintings and curtains. Whole neighbourhoods became reflective. Louis XIV, the "Sun King," built a palace at Versailles with so many mirrors it was scary. One step inside and you'd be beside yourself.)

Anyhow, once back in France, Hélène didn't set foot on a ship again. Ten years after Champlain died in 1635, she gave up her chunk of Sam's estate, her little mirror, her surname and just about everything else, when she entered the Ursuline monastery in Paris and became Sister Hélène-de-Saint-Augustin. After a couple of years she left Paris for Meaux (pronounced "Mo," as in "Motown"), where she headed up her own monastery and became a Mother Superior — the only experience of motherhood she ever had. Hélène died in 1654, at age 56, respected by all who knew her, in "odour of sanctity."

"odour of sanctity": People once believed that saints, or persons who were saintly, actually gave off a sweet smell when they died — or when they were dug up after being buried for a while. (Of course, people also thought that your first mouthful of spit in the morning cured snakebite. And boils.)

THE FATHER OF NEW FRANCE?

Sam was known as the Father of New France, what with the settlements and all, but he was never a real father. He and Hélène didn't have children — probably didn't see each other all that much. Nevertheless, Champlain was, for a short time, the proud father of three girls. For several years he'd wanted to adopt some native kids and send them to school in France. But the native parents didn't want to hand their offspring to this hairy old guy from an unknown land across the large water. (Remember what happened to Donnacona's sons?)

However, in 1628, Champlain got his wish — and it came about because of a double homicide. Members of the Montagnais tribe had killed two French settlers a few months earlier, and things were just a little tense. To get back in Sam's good books, the Montagnais showed up at Québec on a cold February day and gave him three girls, aged eleven, twelve and fifteen. Champlain named them *Foi, Espérance* and *Charité* (Faith, Hope and Charity). Foi got restless within weeks and took off for home, but the other girls happily learned to sew and embroider and speak some French and generally behave as the French did. Champlain wrote in his journal, "They perform most neatly, and moreover they are highly civilized."

They were, as it happens, far more civilized than the kings of England and France, a pair of childish oafs who had — tiresomely and yet again — declared war on each other. This was too bad, both for Champlain and the girls. In 1629 the English captured Québec and took Champlain prisoner. He and the girls ended up at Tadoussac, where Champlain asked that the girls be allowed to go to France. The answer was no, mostly because the fellow who called the shots in Tadoussac was Nicolas Marsolet, who had already double-crossed France and Champlain by going over to the English side. For the right amount of money, Nicolas was

your man. Nicolas was not nice. Nicolas was a greedy immoral pig. Nicolas was, in fact, a major sleaze — no other word for it. (Well, there *are* other words, but your parents wouldn't want you reading them.) Anyway, when Tricky Nicky saw Espérance and Charité, his eyes lit up. He thought they'd be fun to have around . . . and his intentions were definitely not honourable.

To keep them, he lied to his English bosses, the Kirke brothers, claiming that if the girls went to France, the Montagnais might get seriously ticked off. The last thing the English wanted was ticked-off natives, so the girls had to stay. Right away they went on a hunger strike, and a few nights later when the Kirkes threw a dinner party, the girls (still on strike) blasted Nicolas. With both barrels.

Espérance told him he was a traitor and a seducer, saying, "If you come near me in the future I shall plunge a knife into your breast." Then Charité piped up: "If I had hold of your heart, I should eat it more readily and with greater spirit than I should eat any of the meats on that table." Champlain later wrote that Marsolet "was shamefaced, and could give no reply other than that they were mad."

The Kirkes still wouldn't let them leave Canada. Just before he sailed to Europe, Champlain gave each girl a rosary and entrusted them to the care of a settler's family in Québec. When he came back in 1633 there was no sign of them. Hope and Charity, like Faith before them, had fled to the forest.

The Huron were called Huron because:

(a) they lived near Lake Huron

(b) everybody has to be called something

(c) they had messy hair

(d) they kept telling the French, "You're on our land! You're on our land!"

ANSWER:

(c) But it needs to be explained. First, the Huron didn't call *themselves* Huron; they called themselves *Ouendat* or *Wendat*, "the people of the peninsula," meaning the Bruce Peninsula near Ontario's Georgian Bay, where they lived. (Wyandotte, near Detroit — and a main road in Windsor, Ontario — comes from the same word.) Second, it was the French who named them Huron, and they didn't mean it as a compliment. In Old French, *hure* meant "head of a beast." Later it meant "head of a wild boar," and later still "ruffian" — a wild, brawling, lawless person. The Wendat wore their hair long, a bit like the hippies of

the 1960s, and to the French it seemed straggly and uncombed, much like the head of a wild boar. Nobody is sure what the Wendat called the French, but we know they thought beards and curls were disgusting, worn only by those whose IQ equalled their shoe size.

VISIONARIES, VILLAGERS, VOYAGEURS

The power elite in Old France wanted three things from New France: cash, colonies and converts to Catholicism. And the greatest of these was cash. To get the cash (from beaver pelts as well as stuff from China — if they could ever figure out how to get there), they had to establish colonies or outposts where the natives could bring their furs. One way to ensure the natives' loyalty (that is, to stop them from trading with the Protestant English and Dutch, who were making moves in what is now New York state) would be to convert them to the one true faith — *their* faith, that is, Catholicism. The call went out: Send in the priests.

The call was answered. Champlain brought the first priests with him in 1615, four *Récollets* ("detached from worldly matters and *re-collected* in God"), who followed the simple rules of St. Francis. They were to go around in rags, eat as little as possible, and love all creatures great and small. This lifestyle didn't catch on too well with the natives, most of whom loved to dress up (or didn't dress at all), ate as much as they could whenever possible, and hated with a ferocious glee. Some souls, however, were successfully saved, especially if they were about to be detached from their bodies. These unfortunates converted on the spot, just to be on the safe side.

One dynamite soul-saver was twenty-nine-year-old Récollet Father Joseph Le Caron, who, on

August 12, 1615, said the first Mass in Canada, up in Huron country beside Nottawasaga Bay. He stayed most of that winter with the Huron, setting up a mission and learning the language. Later he did the same among the Montagnais at Tadoussac, where he taught several natives to read and write French (some people would consider that martyrdom!) and compiled a French-Montagnais dictionary. But after the fall of Québec in 1629, most of the Récollets returned to France to luxuriate in poverty.

The Jesuits had better luck. Dogged, devoted, disciplined to the point of obsessiveness, and often wildly heroic, they delivered the gospel until their dying breaths — of which there was no shortage. From 1632 to 1672, in order to attract more settlers, the Jesuits sent back an annual report, with a really snappy title: *Relation de ce qui s'est passé de plus remarquable aux missions de Pères de la Compagnie de Jésus en la Nouvelle France.* (The working title might have been *Father Knows Best.* Or maybe *Mission Impossible.*)

These reports were weird: one chapter told you how great the country was, and how a *sou*-less peasant or worker from the old country could have

a whole farm, be his own boss, and even pile up a few *livres* for his old age. The next chapter gave you scary details about Iroquois raids and their nightmarish torture of prisoners, how terrified the settlers were all the time, and how you'd be lucky if you made it to old age. So the folks in France didn't exactly rush down to the docks and jump into a boat going west. In the ten years from 1640 to 1650 the European population of New France rose from 375 to 675, an average of only 30 people a year.

If wannabe settlers *did* decide to set sail, who knew if they'd reach the other side of the ocean? The ship might sink, or be stalled by storms. Then the food and water might run out, and the passengers might starve, or get scurvy, or just catch a cold and sneeze themselves into eternity. Until the late 1700s a sea voyage was more like a floating game of Russian roulette: your trip was considered a good one if only one-tenth of the people on board — none of them *you* — died en route. If you booked a cruise back then, it was with Take-A-Chance Travel, featuring Bet-Your-Life Boats, whose motto was: We guarantee* that most of you will arrive alive.

*Maybe

And if they did get to the other side, they sure didn't find Shangri-La or Club Med . . . or even Cleveland. It was not, repeat *not*, a day at the beach. What they found was more like cruel and unusual punishment.

Suppose you're a settler, just arrived from a little town in the south of France, where the temperature is above freezing most of the time and where your neighbours speak your language. You get off the boat — you're one of the lucky ones — and all you see are trees. Tall, solid, ancient, impenetrable trees: maple, oak, birch, elm, with forests of fat pine here and there. *Bonne mère!* Where oh where are you going to plant your veggies?

First you have to get rid of the trees, right? All you have is an axe and a saw, so it takes a while. Like a year. By that time you've cleared two acres (4/5 of a hectare) — about the size of a soccer field. Well, yippee.

Nobody knew quite how big an acre was until 1525 or so. England's Henry VIII decided it was 40 rods long and 4 rods wide, a rod being 51/2 yards — about 5 metres. (Before that, a rod was measured by lining up sixteen men in single file after church on Sunday, and measuring the combined length of all their left feet.)

Then you find out that "cleared" doesn't really mean cleared. The trees are gone but their stumps remain — hundreds of them. You don't have an ox, or a horse, or a backhoe, or a handy box of dynamite. So you just have to wait till the stumps rot, living on whatever you can shoot, catch and gather. Like two or three years. At last you can plough and plant — all by hand, of course — once the weather warms up.

But when the weather warms up so do the black flies and mosquitoes. It's chow time . . . for them. They get themselves into battle formation and launch a massive attack on all fronts. And backs and sides and tops and bottoms, too. You're bugged to the max. You've surrendered so much blood you feel bleached. But — and here's the zinger — you might shed more blood yet, because lurking in the woods, beneath that rock, under that bush, beyond the potato patch, are the Iroquois, eager for your scalp.

So you had to be a really special person to leave the safety and comfort of home and tough it out in the wilderness of Canada. And there were many who did. Some were driven by visions of Almighty God, others by visions of the almighty dollar — or they would have been, if dollars had existed then. Some were driven by a hunger for adventure, others driven simply by hunger.

Here are a few:

Marie Guyart (1599-1672), a.k.a. Marie de l'Incarnation, was married off at seventeen, under protest, to silk worker Claude Martin. She didn't much like it. Fortunately Claude died two years later, leaving Marie with six-month-old Claude Junior. Marie bunked at her folks' place for a while, where she had a mystical vision of bathing in the blood of Christ.

So she gave Junior to her sister, said *adieu*, and joined the Ursuline nuns. Junior ran away from home, and was later found outside the convent screaming, "Give me back my mother!" It didn't happen. Marie dreamed of a country of mountains, valleys and fogs; God told her it was Canada. Off she went, to land at Québec in 1639. She scrimped, starved, suffered, served God and founded the Ursuline order in Canada. She taught native girls

to read, write, count and pray, calling them "the flowers of the wood" and "the delights of my heart." Sublimely spiritual, an inspired speaker and a gifted writer, fluent in two native languages, modest Marie de l'Incarnation is a towering figure in the history of New France.

Junior entered the priesthood and got to be a big chief.

Paul de Chomedey de Maisonneuve (1612-1676) was "a gentleman of virtue and courage," of noble birth (see the *de*, as in Samuel *de* Champlain?). He joined the army at the tender age of thirteen. To keep himself free of sin, he learned to pluck the lute. (I am not making this up.) To further avoid temptation, he resolved to live in "remote places." After reading one of the Jesuit *Relations*, especially the cheery bits, he decided Canada was a suitably remote place. His mission, backed by a bunch of high rollers in Paris, was to found a faith-based colony on Montréal Island, and bring the heathens to God. Or vice versa. He captained a group of fifty or so — soldiers, settlers, a couple of priests, the first Canadian nurse Jeanne Mance — and, after a brutal six-month voyage with three false starts, arrived in Tadoussac in September, 1641.

The folks in Québec didn't fancy the notion of a rival colony upriver and told Paul it was too dangerous. His reply reflects his character: "Sir, . . . my honour is at stake, and . . . I must go up there to start a colony, even if all the trees on that island were to change into so many Iroquois." Paul went on to govern Montréal for thirty years, serving and protecting his little band through tough times and bloody battles. He was brave, loyal, devoted . . . and avoided evil to the last. You can see a monument to his memory in Montréal's Place d'Armes. One of the good guys.

Zacharie Cloutier (1590-1677), master carpenter, pioneer at Beauport (just east of Québec), arrived in 1637. An ordinary guy who worked like a dog, fought with his neighbours, fathered five children, signed his name with an axe-shaped mark, lived long, and is the ancestor of all the Cloutiers in Canada. Without him, and tens of thousands like him, Canada would not have been built.

Eléonore de Grandmaison (1620-1692), adventurous and otherwise capable, had trouble hanging on to husbands. Wed as a teenager and widowed almost right away, she married François de Chavigny, who owned property on the north shore of the St Lawrence, 15 leagues (70 kilometres) from Québec. There the couple, either courageous or crazy, lived from 1645 to 1648, constantly menaced by Iroquois. They then moved to Île d'Orléans, where Eléonore was the first white woman. François died at sea in 1651. Eléonore, already a mother of six, promptly got hitched to Jacques Gourdeau and, in a virtuoso display of multiplication, had four more kids.

In 1663 Jacques was murdered by a servant, who then set the house on fire. Six months later Eléonore got married yet again, to another Jacques (Cailhaut), who managed to stay alive for ten years. Eléonore de Grandmaison lasted another twenty. She was a good businesswoman and kindly landlady to the few Huron left after epidemics and massacres, renting out several acres to them in the 1650s. She was, furthermore, never bored.

In the early days of the colony, there were eight men to every woman. Even considering that Eléonore de Grandmaison did her connubial (look it up) best to finish off four of them, there were still a lot of guys hanging around. Many of them were young, adventurous and poor. They took one look at the hard life of the settler/farmer, shuddered, and promptly ran off to the woods to be *coureurs de bois*. A *coureur de bois* — "runner of the woods" — was an independent fur trader, who ventured by canoe into the north and west, haggled with the natives for beaver pelts, then sold them back at Tadoussac or Québec for a nice profit. It was a great gig. A *coureur de bois* could:

1. be his own boss
2. make a quick buck (or livre)
3. live on the edge
4. eat with his fingers
5. wear the same clothes for six months or so
6. scratch himself whenever and wherever
   he pleased.

His life was one of freedom to the infinite power. Who could resist?

Such fellows paddled and peddled all over the eastern half of the continent, travelling as far west as Lake Superior. (Their counterparts in New York were "bushlopers," from the Dutch words *busse*, "bush," and *loopman*, "runner.") Along the way, the *coureurs* explored the country, discovered its rivers and lakes and revelled in the risks of the raw wilderness. They lived with and learned from the natives, often — and with astounding frequency — "marrying" native women. They mastered many languages and dialects, and formed friendships and alliances vital to later history. The *coureur de bois* — who evolved into the *voyageur*, a licensed employee of a fur trading company — was a major player in the drama of early Canada.

On the other hand, he was often a rowdy, reckless, unwashed, uncombed, aromatic, hell-raising, drunken, rip-roaring, ready-for-a-fight rapscallion — sort of like a wild west cowboy before there *were* wild west cowboys. He also sang, especially when paddling. A favourite lyric, and one of the first Canadian hits, was *"Petit rocher,"* a lugubrious (look that up, too) last lament of a trapper seriously punctured by Iroquois arrows and awaiting a messy death.

Help Wanted

Job Opportunity: Young men, single, healthy, strong, not too tall, eager for adventure, for exciting journeys by canoe to *le pays d'en haut*. Good singing voice an asset.

Risks: Torture, occasional scalping, drowning, bad food, wild beasts, frostbite, upset stomach, paddler's itch, chronic dandruff, fleas.

Life expectancy: 35 years.

Benefits: Wine, women, song . . . and money, in large amounts. Fresh air. Exercise.

Apply to: M. Legrand-Tricheur, FURS 'R' US, Ville-Marie, Canada.

"We'll tan your hides!"

Did you know that . . .

There are more beavers in Canada today than there were when the Europeans first came?

Étienne Brûlé

CAN I GO SHOOT THE RAPIDS? CAN I... HUH, CAN I?

CAN THE CANOE AND GO FIND MORE FURS!

In southern Ontario, there's a Brûlé Park, a Brûlé Lakeway, a Brûlé Trail, a Brûlé Terrace, a Brûlé Gardens and a Brûlé Crescent. Here a Brûlé, there a Brûlé, everywhere a Brûlé-Brûlé, E-I-E-I-O. Just who is Brûlé and how come his name is all over the map? Brûlé is, of course, Étienne Brûlé, and his name is all over the map because his body was. Before there *was* a map.

Étienne was born around 1592, just outside Paris. He popped up in Québec in 1608 and got to know Champlain. At sixteen, Étienne was a wild and crazy guy, the kind no mother would want her daughter to hang with — a real cowboy. A cowboy who wanted to play with the Indians. So he asked Champlain if he could, Champlain said okay, and Étienne scampered happily into the wilderness in 1610, staying the whole winter with the Iroquets, an Algonquin tribe, near the Ottawa River. Maybe. And he was likely the first white guy to shoot the Lachine rapids in a canoe. Or so the story goes.

The name became La Chine around 1670. Here's

why: Explorer and failed priest René-Robert Cavalier de La Salle, hungry for power and glory, and owner of the land around the rapids, set out to find China by way of the Ohio River. He didn't. *Quelle surprise!* When he got home — with a bad cold — people made fun of him, calling his land *La Chine*, or China. Ho-ho.

But back to Brûlé. In June of 1611 he came back, speaking native like a native. Champlain wrote about the reunion: "I also saw my French boy who came dressed like an Indian. He was well pleased with the treatment received from the Indians, according to the customs of their country, and explained to me all that he had seen . . . and what he had learned. . . ." So there was a new kid on the block: interpreter, go-between, *coureur de bois* and bigtime cog in the fur trade machine.

Étienne got hooked on native life and spent much of the next twenty years with the Huron, accepted as a blood brother. (Also as a "husband" — several times.) Like a sailor with a girl in every port, Brûlé had a girl at every portage. Later on, Champlain got really uptight about Étienne's free and easy lifestyle, writing that Brûlé " . . . was recognized as being very vicious in character, and much addicted to women." In fact, what really ticked him off was that Brûlé had started working for the Kirke brothers, those hated English merchants, encouraging the First Folks to trade with

By the way, Lachine wasn't Lachine then. It was Sault-St-Louis. (In the 17th century the word *sault* or *saut* meant "falls" or "rapids.")

them rather than with the French.

In the course of his life Étienne was the first European to see four of the Great Lakes — Ontario, Erie, Huron and Superior. He was the first to view the copper mines north of Lake Superior, worked so long ago by the First Folks. He was the first to stand on the spot that became Toronto. Boisterous, adventurous, independent, exuberant — a wild and crazy guy indeed — Brûlé's death was, like his life, a Gothic thriller. Despite his long friendship with the Bear tribe of the Huron, sometime in 1633 they murdered him. Nobody knows why. Then they cooked him. Then they ate him. (That day the *specialité du jour* was *"Étienne — brûlé."*)

Bad move. Not just for Étienne, but for the Bear tribe, too. And we're not talking indigestion here. The Bear felt haunted by Brûlé's spirit. Misery spread. So did suspicion. So did epidemics. The village was abandoned. The Bear left their home ground and dispersed, sure that Brûlé had cursed them forever.

WOULD YOU REPEAT THAT, PLEASE?

Brûlé's mastery of native languages and dialects has to rank as one of the wonders of the New World. They are fiendishly difficult. (Even harder than English, which is so weirdly unphonetic that you can spell "fish" as *ghoti: gh* as in rou*gh,* *o* as in w*o*men, *ti* as in atten*ti*on.) Étienne must have had an acrobatic tongue, perfect pitch and the ears of an owl. He didn't have a dictionary, of course: before the Europeans showed up, the First Folks had no written works, although they sometimes used picture writing to get the message across. (See sample on page 158.) Even then it might take a few wild guesses to fill in the blanks.

Suppose, just for fun, you're whisked back to Brûlé's time, and you want to have a chat with a native. Here's what you might face:

1. Five states of inanimate — non-living — matter or objects, as in rock, lightning, canoe, tomahawk, mud.
2. Some words and pronunciations used only by females.
3. Meanings of words can change according to the pitch and tone of your voice, and which syllable you stress (just as in Chinese languages).
4. Hundreds of different verb forms, depending on who says it, when it's said, to whom it's said, and

where it's said; on whether it's in the far past, the near past, the present, the future, or the far future; and on whether it could have happened, is certain to happen, or is unlikely to happen. Whew!

Here are a couple of examples from modern Mohawk. First you have to know that one syllable in a Mohawk word is always louder than the others and marked with an accent. If the accent is ´ , your tone rises; if it's ` , your tone falls. The symbol : tells you to hold the vowel longer, and the symbol ' means you make a little catch in the back of your throat, like the one in the middle of "Oh-oh." (It's called a "glottal stop.")

tóka' = if ; *tó:ka'* = I don't know; *tóhka'* = several
oká:ra' = story; *okà:ra'* = eye
onón:ta' = hill; *onòn:ta'* = milk

Whew again! Wonder how you say: "I'm exhausted!"

Translation (bolded words indicate the pictures):
Home (I) **leave** (to go on a journey in a) **canoe**
(to be gone for) **ten** (days). (I arrive on an) **island**
(on which live) **two families** (and there I meet a)
friend.   **We go together in my canoe to** (another)
island (where) **we hunt with bows and arrows**.
(We kill a) **sea lion**. (We start our) **return** (journey
and) **my friend returns in the canoe with me**.
    (After) **ten** (days) (I arrive) **home**.

Trail Mix

Priests and *voyageurs*, collecting souls and skins respectively, often travelled with First Folks and followed their ways — some delightful, some not. Their cuisine could be hard to swallow (tee-hee), and priests in particular were appalled. Also queasy. Here, from one historian, are the lurid specifics:

Between Montréal and Huronia the Indians had supplies of corn cached at intervals of two-days' travel. . . . they existed on two meals a day of *sagamité* [from Cree *kisakumitew*, "the broth is hot"], corn ground between two stones and boiled into mush . . . ; mixed in with it were any dirt or insects . . . on the stones. If any birds or fish were caught, they were just thrown into a pot and boiled without being [cleaned]; small animals had their fur seared off in the fire before they were tossed in. As the stew came to a boil, the feathery, furry scum was scooped off the top; then everyone dipped in. If a war party returning home with prisoners ran short of food, one of the captives was knocked on the head, quickly butchered, and boiled in the kettle.

ANYONE FOR SECONDS ?

THE SKINNY ON SCALPING

Scalping — the removal of an enemy's scalp, including the hair — wasn't confined to the natives of North America. It was common about 2500 years ago among the ancient Persians, the Scythians of south-western Asia, and some of the bloodier folks in Siberia. And not all North American tribes practised it. Those who did, who lived mostly in the east around the St. Lawrence valley, didn't do it all that much. They preferred to take the whole head — it looked terrific hanging on the tipi — or the hands and feet. But if you were far from your home camp, it was a lot easier to take just the scalp. (How many body parts could you carry, especially when you didn't have any pockets?)

Scalping was a rite of passage, a demonstration of valour in battle — and a tactic to horrify the heck out of the palefaces. Which is ironic, not to mention hypocritical. After all, these were the same palefaces who got a kick out of crucifixion, chuckled while setting people on fire, and often performed unnecessary bowel extraction without anaesthetic. Like, we're talking world-class torturers here.

At any rate, the white guys didn't stay horrified for long. They started scalping, too, and then, with that good old North American know-how, turned it into a business. The Puritans were the first to see

TOO GRUESOME TO CARTOON!

the possibilities. To decrease what they saw as the "surplus" native population (which, to some nasty people, was *all* of it), they actually offered money for scalps. A new class of bounty hunters was born. The English paid money for the scalps of the French and their aboriginal allies. The French did the same for scalps of the English and their supporters. Age and sex didn't matter: old grandmothers, young men, mothers with babies — it was off with the tops of their heads. You made more money if you scalped grown men, though. At one time in Massachusetts a native warrior's scalp was worth £50, while the scalp of a woman or a child under fourteen would net you only half that amount.

Many white men, and even some women, actually made scalping a career, until they'd saved up enough to get married, or buy a plough, or a couple of horses, or a few acres of (formerly native) land, or new curtains for the living room. What's more, everybody thought it was a super idea — especially the preachers, who not only encouraged it, but also invested in scalping parties and got part of the profits, all the better to glorify God.

The sixth commandment? Forget about it! Amen.

DYING BREATH DEPT.

The Jesuit priests, nicknamed "blackrobes" by the natives, are nothing if not persistent. No sooner does one get transferred — by ship to France or by tomahawk to dwell in the house of the Lord forever — than another pops up, like ducks in a shooting gallery. You'd swear they have a death wish. No matter what the obstacle, they keep on keeping on, trying to persuade the heathen that the Christian God is way better than Gitchi Manitou. But the First Folks have reservations. (Ho-ho.) A Huron elder, perplexed by the priests' single-mindedness, and finding the idea of Hell utterly laughable, remarks to Father Jean de Brébeuf: "Do you not see that, as we inhabit a world so different from yours, there must be another heaven for us, and another road to reach it?"

Brébeuf arrives in New France in 1625. After a few months roaming around with the Montagnais in eastern Québec, where he discovers mosquitoes, black flies, dirt, sleeping on bare earth, native porridge, and kneeling in a canoe for twelve hours at a stretch, he leaves for Huron country. There he learns the language and spreads the Good News until 1629, when the Kirke brothers take over Québec. All the French who live there, and all the missionaries, go home to the motherland, except Madame Hébert and her kids.

Back again in 1633, Brébeuf picks up where he left off, and in his spare time writes a Huron dictionary and grammar.

When a lethal smallpox epidemic hits in 1640, and 15,000 Huron die, the natives blame the priests (not without cause), and just about wreck the little mission near

Bites
Black Flies
Blackrobes
Blisters
Blood
Burns

what is now called Orillia, beating up Brébeuf in the process. Does this scare him off? No way! Following a few years with the so-called Neutrals, a peaceful Iroquoian tribe near Hamilton (known to the Huron as *Attiwandaronk*, "people who talk funny"), back he goes again.

Things seem serene — but trouble is afoot. The Iroquois, by now thoroughly annoyed by the French and their hangers-on, carry out hit-and-run raids, each bolder and more deadly than the last. Fear spreads faster than the pox. The Huron are too scared to go to Québec, even though they've been offered protection and shelter there. Several missionaries are captured, tortured and/or killed, and an entire village of Neutrals is wiped out.

On March 16, 1649, just before dawn, a band of 1000 Iroquois descends on the Huron mission. Blood stains the remnants of snow; blood darkens the green and tender grass. Brébeuf and Father Gabriel Lalemant, although they have a chance to escape, refuse to leave. It's as if they stubbornly seek to be martyrs. They are captured and stripped of the hated black robes. Their fingernails are pulled out, and their skin peeled off. And the long slow deaths, at which the Iroquois are so expert, begin. For Brébeuf, it starts at high noon. He lasts until four o'clock.

Lalemant, seventeen years younger than Brébeuf, endures much the same, but three times as long. He dies just before sunrise the next day, after eleven hours of torture, including a couple of refinements Brébeuf was spared: a hatchet is driven into his head and his brains leak out; and

burning coals are jammed into his eyes.

Two hundred and eighty years later, Brébeuf and Lalemant, along with six others, are elevated to sainthood by the Catholic Church. Their beloved mission, now known to us as Sainte-Marie Among the Hurons, is restored by faithful hands. Beneath its soil rest the mortal remains of Father Jean de Brébeuf.

The Huron mission ends with the death of the man who began it. The Huron nation is destroyed, with its few people scattered and forlorn, no longer a partner in the fur trade.

Vive les Voyageurs!

The French lose their foothold in the west. Now the *voyageur* is more important than ever. Whether working for hire or paddling his own canoe, he is the link between Old France and New France, between the known and the unknown — and maybe really rich! — lands of a huge continent.

Every year dozens of *voyageurs* set forth, young men from Montréal, from Trois-Rivières (where one year more than half the men packed up and left), from Cap-de-la-Madeleine, from Batiscan, from Châteauguay, from Québec. For two centuries and more they ranged far and wide, to the western ocean, to the swampy shores of the Mississippi Delta, to the bleak and treeless Arctic, discovering, trading, exploring, drinking, marvelling, partying, dreaming, singing and scratching, preparing the way for all who came after.

Here are a bunch of them:

Daniel Greysolon Dulhut: a top gun in the French army, he arrived in Canada in 1675 at age thirty-six. He blithely ignored orders to stick close to Montréal, and in 1678, with seven *voyageurs* and three slaves (a gift from the Sioux) he travelled west to Lake Superior and the Upper Mississippi (Ojibwa *mici zipi*, "gathering-in of all the waters") to collect dead beavers. He built trading posts on Lake Superior, Lake Nipigon (Ojibwa *anemebegong,*

"continuous water," i.e., you can't see the other side) and Detroit (French *étroit*, "strait"). Later on he got gout in his big toe, hobbled around his Montréal living-room for ten years, and died in 1710. The city of Duluth, Minnesota, was named after him, by somebody with a shaky grasp of orthography (look it up).

Just in Case You're Wondering #1 . . .

A *coureur de bois* worked for himself, buying stuff to trade for beaver, selling the beaver and keeping the money. The *voyageur* worked for a company or a fat cat merchant, trading company stuff for beaver, bringing the beaver back to the company (or fat cat) and getting a salary or part of the money. But sometimes a *coureur de bois* worked for a trading company, and sometimes a *voyageur* worked for himself. Glad we cleared *that* up.

Claude Greysolon de La Tourette: Daniel's kid brother (twenty years younger), Claude was the boss of the Nipigon post, where he made a bundle in the beaver business. He went back to France and lived it up. Once, when his home town of Lyon ran

out of funds, he was so rich he gave them the huge sum of 10,800 *livres*. Mind you, part of this was somebody *else's* money: he never repaid 4000 *livres* he borrowed in Canada — until he got dragged into court in 1716 and had to cough it up.

Nicolas Perrot: Barely fifteen when he came to Canada in 1660 with a couple of Jesuit missionaries, Nicky was a quick study, mastering several native languages faster than a speeding preposition. He was an interpreter and *voyageur* for thirty years, and even wrote a book, *Mémoires sur les mœurs, coustumes et relligion des sauvages de l'Amérique Septentrionale*. (By the way, he was NOT the Nicolas Perrot who tried to poison La Salle — we'll talk about him in Book Two.) He forged strong and enduring alliances with many tribes, and he was a faithful and respected friend to the natives, who smoked ceremonial pipes with him and regarded him as a *sachem*, or chief, a rare honour. One of the good guys. But he was lousy with money: he was always up to his eyeballs in debt, maybe because he and wife Madeleine had eleven children. Finally Nick went broke, and Madeleine, not surprisingly, went insane.

Just in Case You're Wondering . . . #2

Why are they "Vile Voyageurs" in the title of this book? Good question. (They weren't all that vile, even though the word can mean dirty, messy and smelly. Which a lot of them were.) Well, it had to be alliterative (look it up) and all the other suitable "v" words — venturesome, vainglorious, victorious — were too darned long to fit on the cover.

(Author's personal favourites: "verminiferous," infested with bugs; "vinomadefied," soaked in wine.)

Henri Tonty: A cousin of the Greysolon brothers, Henri was born about 1650. (With two hands.) Twenty-four years later, after six years as a soldier, he had only one. During a battle in Sicily against the Spaniards, a grenade blew off his right hand and he was taken prisoner. This didn't slow him down a bit. He was out of the pokey in six months, after being exchanged for the Sicilian governor's son. Then he got himself another hand, made of metal and leather, with a usefully vicious hook at the end of it (think Captain Hook or Edward Scissorhands), strapped it on, picked up a pension of 300 *livres* (with the new hand, of course), and reported for duty. When that particular war ended, he signed on as lieutenant to René-Robert Cavelier de La Salle (more about him in Book Two, too). La Salle had just got the go-ahead to open up Illinois (the country of the *Illini*, Algonquian for "warriors") and to explore the Mississippi. So off they went, landing at Québec in 1678.

For the next twenty-five years Henri just never stopped moving. Here's part of his itinerary: Michilimackinac; Sault Ste Marie; Utica, Illinois; Chicago; Green Bay, Wisconsin (then called "Bay of Stinks"), en route to which their canoes were wrecked and they had to live on wild garlic dug up from under the snow (the hook came in handy); the Gulf of Mexico; Louisiana (named for Louis XIV); Manhattan island; Niagara Falls; Texas; Peoria, Illinois; the mouth of the Arkansas river. Whenever Tonty stayed in one place for a while, he established trade with the local tribes, and made a few dollars for himself. The natives, who called him *Bras-de-Fer* ("Iron Arm"), were blown away by his endurance, determination and courage. Almost single-handedly

NOW, IF I CAN JUST GET THIS INTO MY MOUTH WITHOUT POKING MY EYE OUT!

(heh-heh) he brought about a peaceful and profitable co-existence with the indigenous folk of the southwest. But in 1704, a ship from Havana docked at Fort Biloxi, Mississippi, with a deadly stowaway — yellow fever. In September, 54-year-old Henri Tonty — soldier, explorer, trader, *voyageur* — who had overcome so much, discovered so much, achieved so much — died from a mosquito bite.

Just in Case You're Wondering . . . #3

And where the heck are those famous *voyageurs*, Radishes and Gooseberries? So nicknamed by generations of students trying to be funny, **Pierre Esprit-Radisson** (French *radis*, "radish") and his brother-in-law **Médard Chouart des Grosseilliers** (French *groseille*, "currant" or "gooseberry"), led lives right out of *Adventure Comics*. Danger! Discovery! Daring Deeds! These guys did it all — in fact, they did so much there's no room for them in this book. You'll have to wait for Book Two.

There's a Book Two? You betcha. Read The Closing Bit.

The Closing Bit

Told you so. Canadian history's not boring at all. Okay, so there are no car chases or explosions. (Not yet, anyway. Who knows what'll happen in Book Two?) But there's a ton of agony, blood, power, money and murder. History, you see, is much more than "Once there were people and they did stuff." History is "Once there were brave, foolish, heroic, cowardly, adventurous, cruel, greedy, romantic, determined, nutty and magnificent people — and they did unbelievable, terrible, splendid and awesome stuff."

History is really *biography* — stories about people. People who walked where you now walk, heard the birds you now hear, beheld the mountains and valleys and lakes and rivers you now behold. People like your mom, and your best friend down the street, and your pesky little sister, and the cousin who's so gross, and the aunt nobody talks about except in whispers, and your great-grandfather, who died in World War II and got a medal your dad keeps in a blue velvet box on the mantelpiece.

And you.